Yesterday Framed in Today

THE ALDEN
COLLECTION

Isabella Macdonald Alden

Yesterday Framed in Today

CREATION
HOUSE
BOOKS ABOUT SPIRIT-LED LIVING
LAKE MARY, FLORIDA

Creation House
Strang Communications Company
190 North Westmonte Drive
Altamonte Springs, FL 32714
(407) 862-7565

Originally published in 1898

Unless otherwise noted, all Scripture quotations are
from the King James Version of the Bible.

CONTENTS

ABOUT THE AUTHOR

sabella Macdonald Alden, under the pen name "Pansy," exerted a great influence upon the American people of her day through her writings. She also helped her niece, Grace Livingston Hill, get started in her career as a best-selling inspirational romance novelist.

As Grace tells it in the foreword to *Memories of Yesterdays,* her aunt gave her a thousand sheets of typing paper with a sweet little note wishing her success and asking her to "turn those thousand sheets of paper into as many dollars.

"I can remember how appalling the task seemed and how I laughed aloud at the utter impossibility of its ever coming true with *any* thousand sheets of paper. But it was my first real encouragement, the first hint that anybody thought I ever could write. And I feel that my first inspiration came from reading her books and my mother's stories, in both of which as a child I fairly steeped myself."

On another occasion, shortly before Grace's twelfth birthday in 1877, Isabella had been listening to Grace tell a story about two warmhearted children. As she listened, she typed out the story and later had it printed and bound by her own publisher into a little hardback book with woodcut illustrations. She surprised her niece with the gift on her birthday. That was Grace's first book.

Isabella Macdonald was born November 3, 1841, in Rochester, New York, the youngest of five daughters. Her father, Isaac Macdonald, was educated and was deeply interested in everything religious. Her mother, Myra Spafford Macdonald, was the daughter of Horatio Gates Spafford (1778-1832), author and inventor. Isabella's uncle, Horatio Gates Spafford Jr., penned the popular hymn "It Is Well With My Soul" after learning that his wife had survived a tragic shipwreck; his four daughters were lost at sea.

Isabella was taught at home on a regular daily basis by her father. As her guide and friend, he encouraged her to keep a journal when she was young and to develop a natural affection for writing. Under his direction she acquired the ease and aptness of expression for which her writings became known. When she was only ten, the local weekly newspaper published her composition titled "Our Old Clock," a story that was inspired by an accident to the old family clock.

That first published work was signed "Pansy." Isabella acquired that name partly because pansies were her favorite flower and partly because of a childhood episode. She tried to help her mother get ready for a tea party by picking all the pansies from the garden to decorate the tea table. Not knowing the flowers were to be tied into separate bouquets and placed at each lady's place, Isabella carefully removed all the stems.

Years later, while teaching at Oneida Seminary, from which she had earlier graduated, Isabella wrote her first novel, *Helen Lester*, in competition for a prize. She won fifty dollars for submitting the manuscript that explained the plan of salvation so clearly and pleasantly that very young readers would be drawn into the Christian fold and could easily follow its teachings.

Isabella wrote or edited more than two hundred published works, including short stories, Sunday school lessons and more than a hundred novels. She had only one manuscript rejected. At one time her books sold a hundred thousand copies annually with translations in Swedish, French, Japanese, Armenian and other languages.

She usually wrote for a young audience, hoping to motivate youth to follow Christianity and the Golden Rule. The themes of her books focused on the value of church attendance; the dangers lurking in popular forms of recreation; the duty of total abstinence from alcohol; the need for self-sacrifice; and, in general, the requirements, tests and rewards of being a Christian.

Reading was strictly supervised for young people in that day, and Sunday schools provided many families with reading material. Thus, Isabella's fiction received wide circulation because of its wholesome content.

Furthermore, readers liked her books. Her gift

for telling stories and her cleverness in dreaming up situations, plus just a little romance, held the interest of readers young and old. Isabella was known for developing characters who possessed an unwavering commitment to follow the Master. She portrayed characters and events that anyone might encounter in a small American town during the last quarter of the nineteenth century.

A writer in *Earth Horizon* (1932) acknowledged that "whoever on his ancestral book shelves can discover a stray copy of one of the Pansy books will know more, on reading it, of culture in the American eighties [1880s] than can otherwise be described."

Isabella believed wholeheartedly in the Sunday school movement. She edited a primary quarterly and wrote primary Sunday school lessons for twenty years. From 1874 to 1896 she edited *The Pansy*, a Sunday magazine for children, which included contributions from her family and others. An outgrowth of the magazine was the Pansy societies which were made up of young subscribers and aimed at rooting out "besetting sins" and teaching "right conduct."

For many years she taught in the Chautauqua assemblies and, with her husband, was a graduate of what was called the Pansy Class, the 1887 class of the Chautauqua Literary and Scientific Circle— the first book club in America. The Chautauqua assemblies were an institution that flourished in the late nineteenth and early twentieth centuries. They combined popular education with entertainment in the form of lectures, concerts and plays and were often presented outside or in a tent.

Throughout her career Isabella took an active interest in all forms of religious endeavors, but her greatest contributions came in her writings. She wanted to teach by precept and parable the lessons her husband taught from the pulpit, in Bible class and in the homes of his parishioners. Her writing was always her means of teaching religious and moral truths as she understood them, and her method was to tell a story.

Her husband, Gustavus Rossenberg Alden, was a lineal descendant of John Alden, one of the first settlers in America. He graduated from Auburn Theological Seminary and was ordained soon after his marriage to Isabella in 1866. He served as a pastor in churches in New York, Indiana, Ohio, Pennsylvania, Florida and Washington, D.C. The Aldens moved from place to place for health reasons and to be near their son, Raymond, during his years of schooling and teaching.

Amidst her many and varied responsibilities as a minister's wife, a mother and a prolific author, Isabella found time to play a significant role in her son's career as a university professor, an author and a scholar in Shakespearean literature.

Her final years were marked by a series of trials. In 1924, after fifty-seven years of marriage, Isabella's husband died. In that same year her last remaining sister, Marcia Macdonald Livingston, Grace's mother, died. A month later her only son, Raymond, died.

About two years later she fell and broke her hip. Although in much pain and discomfort she continued writing until the end. Her final letters were filled with thoughts of going "Home": "Isn't it blessed to realize that one by one we shall all gather Home at last to go no more out forever! The hours between me and my call to come Home grow daily less...."

Isabella Macdonald Alden died August 5, 1930, at the age of eighty-nine in Palo Alto, California, where she and her husband had moved in 1901.

The following year *Memories of Yesterdays*, her last book, edited by her niece, was published. In the foreword Grace describes her aunt:

"I thought her the most beautiful, wise and wonderful person in my world, outside of my home. I treasured her smiles, copied her ways and listened breathlessly to all she had to say....

"I measured other people by her principles and opinions and always felt that her word was final. I am afraid I even corrected my beloved parents sometimes when they failed to state some principle or opinion as she had done."

As Grace was growing up and learning to read, she devoured her aunt's stories "chapter by chapter. Even sometimes page by page as they came hot from the typewriter; occasionally stealing in for an instant when she left the study, to snatch the latest page and see what had happened next; or to accost her as her morning's work was done, with 'Oh, have you finished another chapter?'

"And often the whole family would crowd around, leaving their work when the word went around that the last chapter of something was finished and going to be read aloud. And how we listened, breathless, as she read and made her characters live before us."

May her characters come to life for you as you read this new release in the Alden Collection.

Deborah D. Cole

THE CHARACTERS

David Holman
Frances Holman — David's sister
Margaret Holman — David's sister
Hannah Holman — David's mother
Ezra Holman — David's father
Philip Nelson — friend to David and Frances
Felix Masters — governor's nephew
Miriam Brownlee — David's betrothed
Lillian Brownlee — Miriam's aunt
Mr. Rothwell — a local aristocrat
Mrs. Symonds — widowed sister of Mr. Rothwell
Mary Rothwell — younger sister of Mr. Rothwell
John Brownlee — Miriam's cousin
Mr. Compton — Miriam's visitor
Miss Masters — sister of Felix Masters
Joe Andrews — a town resident
Katherine Brownlee — Miriam's mother

CHAPTER I

WE HAVE
HEARD THE FAME
OF HIM

ay I, the writer of this book, offer in its opening chapter a word of explanation to my readers?

I think you are about to read something that is unlike anything else now in print. No rules pertaining to history or chronology will apply to it. And it is crowded with anachronisms, the only excuse for them being that they are intentional.

For a set purpose that I have tried to carry out, dates and periods of time have been deliberately confused. Also, let me frankly confess to having arranged on paper that which in real life could not be; that is, our present state of civilization has been depicted as if the New Testament never came into being. In other words, I have taken this present time, with its railroads and telegraphs and phonographs and electric lights and whatnot, and lifted into it from out of the historic past a central figure — *the* central figure of all time, the One without whose coming we would not even have counted time as we do now — the Man Christ Jesus.

I have conceived of Him, however, as walking the streets of our cities meeting people who have knowledge of the Old Testament only, though they act and think like the religious people of today. I have imagined such people coming in contact with this central Light, as it shone on earth centuries ago, and treating it in the same spirit that men and women treated it then; the spirit in which undoubtedly many would receive Him now if He were to come again in the same humble, local way.

My object in making this effort — no, on second thought I will leave you to discover my object. If you fail in finding it soon, and sharply defined, I shall have signally failed in my effort.

I want simply to ask you to read carefully and with unprejudiced eyes.

With that brief explanation, I turn to my story.

Mrs. Holman moved about the room with an evident unrest upon her. She opened and closed doors and drawers and boxes with no apparent purpose and in other ways showed a perturbed spirit that was very unlike her usual quiet self.

She glanced nervously and often toward a door that stood ajar, from behind which could be heard a murmur of voices. At intervals she entered the room where the talkers were and engaged in the conversation, returning even more disturbed.

At the extreme end of the room by a south window sat a young woman in a neat house dress, sewing busily. She was a pure-faced, sweet-eyed young woman with an abundance of brown hair that waved low on her forehead. She was almost too young to be called a woman, yet there was about her such an atmosphere of womanhood that one disliked to call her simply a girl.

"Frances is a very womanly girl," said those who were intimate with her, thus compromising between the two words, while comparative strangers had described her as "a sweet, girlish-looking woman."

Her cheeks were pinker this morning than was natural, although they had generally a healthful glow. A close observer would have noted that the hand which held the swift-moving needle trembled a little as she arrested it from time to time to arrange her work. Her eyes also expressed, not trouble, like her mother's, nor even anxiety; they simply suggested that her heart was throbbing with an interest she was carefully holding in check.

During one of the mother's absences from the room, the door leading into the hall opened suddenly, and Margaret Holman entered. Whatever this young girl did was done with suddenness. It seemed sometimes as though she fairly rushed at life and tore its blessings from its hands with an excitement that almost frayed the garments of the blessings.

"Margaret lives too fast," said certain of her friends. "She will use up all her energy and be an old woman exhausted with life years before her time."

It is difficult to describe a girl like Margaret Holman. For that matter, it is difficult to describe anybody. What have hair and eyes and features, regular or irregular, to do with it? Everybody has eyes and lips and a nose apiece. Whether the eyes be blue or gray and the nose be Roman or a trifle turned up makes much less difference than we are inclined to imagine. It is, of course, the subtle something behind all these, which one never attempts to describe, that repels or attracts or perhaps awakens only indifference.

There shall be no attempt at this point to describe Margaret Holman other than to say that the excitement which was being held in check by her sister fairly blazed in the girl's expressive face.

"How can you sit there and sew just as usual!" she exclaimed. "I believe if you had received word of an earthquake occurring tomorrow that would tear this house from its foundations, you would still draw that needle back and forth and take those little bits of stitches. It would drive me wild!"

"Which?" asked Frances. "The knowledge of the earthquake or the sewing?"

"Both. How can you be so still when we are all wrought up? Something ought to be done. You should talk to David. He will listen to you if he will to anybody in the world."

The needle flew in and out, faster, if possible, than before; but the worker remained silent. Only a slightly deepening flush on her cheek indicated that she had heard.

"Why don't you speak?" asked Margaret impatiently. "Say *something*. If you don't, I shall scream. Frances Holman, why don't you go and tell them it is impossible?"

"I cannot," Frances said at last, dropping her work and looking fully at her sister. "I cannot take such a risk."

"I don't understand. Doesn't all the risk lie in his

carrying out this wild idea? I am sure you could prevent it, and yet you sit there and talk about risk! I believe in my heart that you want him to try it!"

The work was back again in the elder sister's fingers, the needle making good progress. At this last sentence the color rushed to her forehead. But her voice, when she spoke again, was low and controlled.

"I am only too glad, dear, that it is not a question for me to decide. We must remember that David is not a boy to be controlled, but a man with such a burden to bear as you and I cannot understand. What must it be to lie year after year in that one room? It is worse than death, infinitely; it would be for me. Sometimes it seems to me as though I could not bear it for him any longer."

Margaret turned away abruptly to hide her tears. She stood for some moments with her back to her sister, then, half turning, spoke more quietly. "I know all that, of course. Don't we all know what you have been to him through these years? I don't suppose I realize it fully, by any means. But ever since I was ill for five weeks I have understood it better. Still, what has that to do with the present question? He is bracing himself up for a terrible effort, which, if he lives through it — and I know Mother is afraid he won't — will only result in a terrible disappointment."

Once more the sewing dropped, and Frances clasped her hands so tightly that her nerves tingled with the pain as she asked, "Isn't there a possibility that he might be helped?"

"Frances!" It was the only word her sister spoke, but it seemed to the girl almost like a blow.

She went on hurriedly. "I know all you would say. But remember what we have heard within a few weeks, what we are constantly hearing. Do you forget Mrs. Ames? She was very ill indeed, they said."

"Oh, 'they said'! If you are going to quote the gossip of the street, there is an end to common sense. Mrs. Ames, at best, is a woman who imagines herself ill enough to die if she has but a toothache. As for crediting for a moment the wild stories that are afloat about her, Frances, I am astonished at you! Is Philip responsible for this state of mind?"

But Frances was evidently not accustomed to being addressed in this way. She looked steadily into her sister's excited eyes as she said with dignity, "Never mind Philip, if you please. There is no occasion to bring his name into our talk."

"I beg your pardon," said the impetuous girl, her face aflame. "I did not mean to say anything disagreeable. But I want to ask one question: If Father had heard your words just now, what would he have said? For Father's sake, if for nothing else, you ought to use your influence. If he were here, you know he would not permit this for a moment. And in his absence — "

"In his absence," interrupted Frances, still with dignity but quite gently, "I cannot assume his responsibilities. The truth is, dear, that David has been ill so long that we have all learned to speak of him as though he were a child under our control, instead of a man of thirty. Even Father, remember, would have no right to control his movements."

Margaret tapped her foot impatiently. "Do you know that seems like nonsense," she said quickly. "So long as David is watched over and cared for like a child, I think he owes it to Father and Mother to follow their advice. He has been quite willing to do so, I am sure, and would be now if he hadn't lost his senses over this excitement. Those young men have talked to him until he doesn't know what he thinks. I must say that they take a good deal upon themselves, coming here to urge the claims of an entire stranger, when we have a family physician in whom we have complete confidence. I wish Father were at home, or Philip. When is he coming? I am sure he would not allow any movement so wild as this."

"I do not know when he will come, and I do not think he would interfere if he were here. Neither will I. It may sound strange to you, but I mean it when I say that I dare not use my influence. Our brother has suffered enough without our trying to treat him as though he were reduced to mental as well as physical helplessness. He has deliberately resolved to make this supreme effort, and I dare not open my lips to try to prevent it."

Margaret turned away impatiently just as her mother re-entered the room.

"Frances," she said, dropping into a chair near her daughter, "will you not try once more to get David to listen to reason? I fear for the consequences of this excitement. Those young men must see how much I want them to go away. What right have they to invade our home and work my poor boy into a fever?"

There was a moment of painful silence, then Frances spoke low. "Mother, I shall have to say to you as I did to Margaret that I dare not interfere. David has set his heart upon this, and the consequences of disappointment are more to be dreaded than the effort."

"Yes," said Mrs. Holman quickly, "that is what I feel. If his poor body could bear such an ordeal, what of afterward, when he is back again in the old place? Oh, it is cruel, *cruel!"*

She hid her face in her hands, and Frances sat in troubled silence again. After a moment she spoke very gently, "Dear Mother, very strange things are happening in the city. Don't you remember what we have heard within a few days? How can we know but that — "

"We can know that a great many people are being deluded by Satan!" exclaimed Mrs. Holman. "I didn't think you could be carried away by a cruel and wicked delusion. What will your father say? Oh, if only he were at home!"

The cause of all this solicitude and distress can be given in a few words. David Holman, the son of the house, was a hopeless, helpless invalid. The large, bright room where he lay had been his world ever since he was twenty-three, and he was now nearing his thirtieth birthday. During much of this time he had suffered racking pain, being unable to bear a movement from his bed to his invalid chair except at the expense of hours of torture. Finally a couch of peculiar pattern had been constructed for his use, and no attempt had been made to move him to any other. Here he had lain day after day and year after year, being tenderly cared for. He had been borne with patiently in his most irritable hours; entertained when his nerves could endure it; soothed and petted like a suffering child when that treatment was what he needed.

The habit of the house had been to think and speak of him as though he were the peculiar blessing of their lives, instead of being what he had been — a wild, reckless boy whose uncontrolled will had brought him at last to the narrow world where he could only lie and wait.

He was never by word or look reminded of this.

By common consent the family had ignored the
past, but it will be well understood that the young
man himself was unable to do so. How much of his
pain grew out of the fact that he had brought himself to this condition, only he and his God knew.

Of course, during all these years no effort nor
expense had been spared in securing the most
skillful medical treatment. More than once, in the
earlier years, the hopes of the entire family had
been raised to the highest pitch, only to be brought
low again when the new treatment failed utterly.

By degrees the family settled into realizing there
was nothing for the idolized son and brother but to
wait until the earthly tabernacle could be put off.
Many hours were spent in secret, weeping and praying for the beloved one, that when that time came he
might be prepared. It seems strange to record the
fact, but fact it was, that, near as he had been to
death, hopeless as he was in life, he yet did not for
years attempt any preparation for that other world
which alone could have any hope for him.

To his sister Frances this condition of things had
seemed far more terrible than the bodily suffering,
and for weeks together her prayer for him had
been one prolonged cry for mercy. There came a
time when he seemed somewhat changed — less
indifferent to all religious conversation, less irritable when her words became what he used to call
personal. He said very little indeed on the subject.
But that little, if not encouraging, was certainly
less discouraging, and the sister, who was his chief
attendant, began to have a trembling hope that he
had found, or was finding, God.

Then suddenly into their quiet home had come a
strange, new influence, a bewilderment, a hope, or
a delusion. They knew not how to name it.

IT WAS A TRUE
REPORT WHICH
I HEARD IN
MINE OWN LAND

he Holman family, because of their affliction and the constant strain upon them of anxiety and care, lived a very quiet life. They mingled very little even with their neighbors and avoided society almost entirely. Yet their home was near the city, and all news of importance reached them sooner or later. At the time in which our story opens, news of a very strange and startling nature engrossed the minds of the public.

There had come to the city at intervals during the season a man who seemed, if one might judge by results, to be a physician of no common order. He was an entire stranger to the neighborhood. But very soon after his first visit remarkable stories be-

gan to circulate as to his power over disease and
pain and, indeed, over trouble of almost any sort.
The most amazing reports had reached the Holmans of the man's ability to cure those who had
been for years considered incurable; and this, not
with a long and expensive process of medical treatment, but with a touch, a word, sometimes only a
look.

Of course, the city was divided as to its opinions. Many sneered at all the stories as baseless
follies. They affirmed that the cures were performed on the bodies of those who had diseased
imaginations only; having imagined themselves
ill, they could on occasion, of course, as easily
imagine themselves well. There were some who
shook their heads and looked mysterious and
hinted that there was something strange and unnatural, not to say "uncanny," about it all.

Most people believed in the existence of an evil
spirit, and it had never been proved that he had
not his emissaries in human flesh. Immediately
there arose those who affirmed that to cure human
pain and relieve misery and give peace where before had been unrest was certainly not the work of
evil spirits; but there were answers ready for such.
Satan, it was said, knew enough in these days to
make of himself an "angel of light" when occasion
demanded. So the city was divided, and excitement ran high.

In the little home on the outskirts of the city,
where our interest centers, it had not been supposed that there were held other opinions than
those advanced by the grave-faced, often stern father.

"We will have nothing to do with such matters,"
he had said, with the positiveness that charac-

terized him. "Nor do we want people running here
to tell their marvelous tales. It is nothing new. Ever
since the world began there has been some sort of
excitement afloat to make the credulous gape and
also to push the heedless into evil. There always
will be, I suppose, but we don't need to be caught
by it. Just keep away from such unhealthy out-
bursts and avoid the people who are forever talking about them. That has always been my habit,
and it's a good one for my children to copy. No
good ever comes from stepping out of the regular
routine of respectable life. I don't believe in street
preaching or street performing of any kind. Let it
be distinctly understood that I will not have the
names of any of my family connected with excite-
ments like these."

Yet despite this emphatic announcement, and
the apparent assurance which the father felt that in
this, as in other matters, his children would follow
his example, stories of the stranger's marvelous
power did float into the house from time to time.
The few neighbors who continued to be friendly
with the isolated family, and who "ran in" to try to
cheer them in their loneliness, would talk about
what was going on in town.

The mother did not much heed their stories. The
truth is, she was one of those women who believe
that what "Father" thinks is right and best, all the
rest of the world to the contrary notwithstanding.
So she sat quietly at her sewing, smiled incredulously over the marvels, only heard half of the particulars and merely cautioned the girls that they
were not to bother "Father" by repeating any of the
talk.

The younger daughter, however, liked to listen
to the reports; they fed her love of the wonderful.

The details amused her greatly. As often as opportunity offered, despite the father's injunction, she was sure to question until she had drawn out the particulars. She was, however, much too loyal to her father, and perhaps too much like him by nature, to have the slightest interest beyond that of amusement in any of the stories. So much as a hint of their possibly serious character was sure to make her indignant.

As for the elder daughter, she listened to the talk as opportunity offered in utmost quiet. Sometimes her face flushed over the details. She caught her breath occasionally to suppress an exclamation, though of what character it would have been, she kept quite to herself.

Matters were in this state, with the father absent from home on a business trip, when something very much like a bombshell of excitement burst in the quiet cottage.

David, the helpless — who, it was thought, had long ago given up the hope of leaving his room until that solemn day when he should be carried from it coffined — suddenly announced his determination to be carried to town the next time the strange physician visited it. He would see for himself if there was any truth in the stories. If even one-third of them were true, it ought to be possible to have something done for him.

In vain the frightened mother pressed upon him the folly, nay, the utter cruelty, of such an attempt. Had he forgotten the awful agony of the time when they moved him, ever so gently, to his present couch? True, he was in less pain now than he used to be, but that was because he had none of those terrible movings to endure. Did he not remember that even now there were days when the jar caused by persons walking across the room was more than he could bear? How, then, could he think that he could endure the motion of being carried down the street? The more fully she spread it out before him, the more fully she realized his utter folly. Not so David.

"It is no use, Mother," he said. "What you tell me may all be true, and my case is probably, as you say, utterly hopeless. Nevertheless, I mean to make the attempt, even though I should die on the road. The boys will carry me on that newly developed cot in such a way that there will be almost no jar. A great many things can be done now, Mother, that could not when I first lay down in this room. Please, good little Mother, don't try to keep me from making this effort; my whole soul is determined on it. I *must* see this man. You know how long it has been since I have felt any interest in doctors. I don't know why I feel as I do, but I am as determined to carry out this plan as I ever was to do anything in my life. And you remember, don't you, that I used to have a will of my own?"

There was a faint flush of color on his face as he made this reference. Nobody ever reminded him how entirely that will of his had ruined his life, but of course they remembered it.

"Yes," said Mrs. Holman with intensity. "I remember that you had."

It was the nearest she had ever come to a reproach for the blighting of her life as well as his own.

Four young men from town were the prime movers in the matter which was causing the family such anxiety. They had been friends of David since his early boyhood, although two of them were younger than he was by several years. They had

spent many nights together at a time when David's
was the ruling spirit, and he had led them to the
very verge of ruin. It had been well for them that
he had been suddenly laid aside in that quiet room.
The accident had set them to thinking, and, with-
drawn from his influence, they had thought to
such purpose that now they were reckoned as
model young men.

They had never grown entirely away from their
early intimacy with David Holman. As time
passed, and his sufferings grew less, they had been
able to beguile many weary hours for him. Mrs.
Holman had been very grateful to them in the days
gone by. However much the family might with-
draw themselves from others, the house had always been open to these young men.

Within a few weeks, however, it had been discovered that they were all more or less interested
in what Mr. Holman characterized as the "superstition" which was spreading over the country. More
than once he had said that he wished those young
men would cease their attentions to David; if they
were as shallow-brained as their interest indicated,
he would certainly not miss them much.

But the mother had urged on their behalf that
they were young and were of course more or less
curious about all new ideas. She also pointed out
that usually their new ideas quickly became old
ideas and were soon tossed aside. In any case, she
contended, they could do no harm to poor David,
who had so few visitors.

So the young men had come and gone as usual,
until suddenly it was discovered that they had
done harm to David. It was they who had urged
him to that fateful decision to see and hear the dangerous stranger for himself!

On the morning in question, Mrs. Holman left her daughter Frances abruptly, with a sore feeling in her heart that she had failed in the quarter where she had looked for help.

She returned to her son's room in time to hear one of the young men say, "You couldn't have chosen a better day than this, Holman. It is warm, but not unpleasantly so; the air is like wine. I believe the mere getting out into it once more will do you good."

The poor mother turned upon the speaker in only partially suppressed indignation. "I thought you had more sense!" she said sharply. "Do you think we would have kept our son housed all these months if there had been any safe way to avoid it? Don't you know, or have you forgotten, that every effort to move him from that corner even has been followed by hours of agony and then by such exhaustion that we have hung over him, fearing that each breath would be his last? If you understood his condition as I do, you would see the folly of thinking for a moment that he could endure being moved over the rough street. I've heard his father say there's not a worse paved street leading to the city than ours. It is uncomfortable for a well person to ride over it — and impossible for my son."

"Oh, Mrs. Holman!" exclaimed the young man who had taken the role of leader throughout. "Don't think for a moment that we would have him ride like a common mortal. Didn't he tell you we have the very best carrying device possible, invented for just such emergencies? We propose to bring one to the side door, lay his bed on it and carry him ourselves. We shall move very slowly, and we don't believe he'll feel any jar whatever. I assure you, dear lady, we have planned most carefully and feel almost certain of the results."

"So do I!" said the poor mother bitterly. But she said no more. She had done all she could to prevent what she believed to be disaster and had failed. The resolute will which, rightly managed, would have been such a blessing to her son had degenerated into willful obstinacy. But that morning his will awoke from its long lethargy and reasserted itself with more than its former strength; he *would* go.

Nothing but dying on the spot would prevent it, he assured his mother with a smile, which in itself revealed the firm lines of his lips.

Without more ado preparations were made for the trying ordeal. The poor sufferer was a marvel to those who knew him well: He bore the torture of being dressed for the outside world without even a groan and, indeed, with no outward sign of suffering, other than his deathly pallor and the dark lines under his eyes which bore witness to his condition.

His mother hovered about him, pale, tearless, silent, trying to the very last to plan for his comfort. Even when she bent and kissed him good-bye — a long, lingering kiss that her foreboding heart told her might be the last that would meet with any response from him — she held herself to silence. It was not the time for speech; she had said what she could, and his father was not at home.

"It is simply a stretcher!" she said, with white lips, her eyes still tearless, as she came into the house at last. She had seen the strange procession off and looked after it until a bend in the road hid them from view. "I have tried to teach myself to expect to see him carried away from me in his coffin, but I didn't think he would go out to meet it!"

David had been the quietest of subordinates and had meekly done to the best of his poor ability just as he was told. But now he had suddenly reasserted himself, decreeing that none of the family should accompany him on his perilous journey. He tried to explain the reason to his sister Frances, who, though she had said no word to deter him from the effort, begged to go with him.

"No, I can't have that. Mother mustn't go, and no one, not even you, blessed sister that you are, must take her place. Besides, if it should turn out to be nothing — as I constantly remind myself that it probably will — I don't know that I can make myself understood; but I feel that I could not endure the look of one of you for a while. I must go through that ordeal quite alone. I shall live to get back — I feel sure of that. So it is not good-bye."

He had smiled upon her as he spoke, but his face was as white as the face of the dead. After a moment he had added, "Kiss me, Frances, and tell Margaret to come and give me a kiss, not for good-bye, but for hope."

Margaret came with tears streaming from her eyes, protesting and beseeching even then. Then his mother had bent over him and given silently that last, long kiss. The four strong men had carried him out, clearly with infinite tenderness, but still at the cost of infinite pain. Seeing his face, his mother and sisters had rushed after him with frightened murmurings, but after a moment he had opened his eyes and smiled again.

"No, Mother," he said, "I didn't faint, not quite. The pain was really less than I had imagined it. Mother, dear, remember, whatever happens, I *had* to do it. No one is to blame but me. Good-bye."

That was his parting word.

CHAPTER III

WE HAVE HEARD
HIS VOICE
OUT OF THE MIDST
OF THE FIRE

mong all the days of the Holman family's experience — and their lives have been somewhat eventful ones — this day, in which they waited at home, will probably always stand out in vivid solitariness of importance to them.

They tried, each for the sake of the others, to busy themselves somewhat in the usual ways — to speak and act as though life ran for them in its accustomed grooves. But of course they could not even accomplish this outwardly. In the first place, there was that deserted room which for years had not been unoccupied even for a moment. For the first hour Mrs. Holman shut and locked herself

within it. When she came out her face was still
markedly pale. But she was quiet and remained so
for most of the day. The windows of the vacated
room were thrown wide open, and preparations
were made for cleaning it more thoroughly than
was often possible. This, too, had its pain.

"It feels as if there had been a death in the house,
and a funeral!" Margaret said, shivering over the
thought. "It is dreadful to see all the windows
thrown open at once, when we have sheltered him
for so long!"

"Hush!" warned Frances, as she turned to see if
her mother had caught the words. "How can you
be so inconsiderate! Let's not make it harder for
her than it must be, nor for ourselves, for that matter. David is out once more under the wonderful
sky and in the pure air of heaven. We don't know
what it may do for him."

Frances had laid aside her sewing, engrossing as
it had seemed to be all morning, and with much
energy was sweeping, dusting and generally setting in order the downstairs rooms. Despite her
words to Margaret, she had a sense of pain at the
thought that she needn't be careful about opening
and closing doors nor mind draughts nor avoid
noises or jars, as they had all been trained to do.
They had been so used to shaping their most commonplace activities with the comfort of their sick
one in mind — and had expected to continue in
this way until he would be carried from them
never to return — that they could not get away
from a terrible feeling that that hour had come
upon them unawares.

As the long day dragged toward the west, the
nervous strain became almost too much to bear.
Mother and daughters struggled bravely to help

one another. They had plunged into unusual and fatiguing work to try to dull their sensibilities. Later, they tried to absorb themselves in preparing an early tea and having it much more elaborate than usual. Margaret tried to say cheerfully that perhaps Father would be at home by teatime. But her voice faltered painfully before the sentence closed. And Frances, who attempted to respond, stopped in the middle of hers.

They had been on the lookout for the father for several days, but now they could not be sure that they wanted him to come. What if — but there they tried to stop even their thoughts.

"It's very strange," said Mrs. Holman at last, speaking out something of her pain, "that we didn't insist upon going with him. I don't understand how I could have been persuaded into staying away, or how you could, Frances. You are young and strong, and David lets you have your way with him. I don't know why you were so persistently quiet today. You could at least have saved us from this awful strain of waiting. It is cruel!"

"David was so set on going without us," said Frances soothingly, "that it seemed best to yield the point. I wanted to go, but he said he could not bear it. He would not have you go for the world, and he would have no one in your place, Mother."

The mother's face worked painfully over this token of her place in her son's heart.

Frances continued, "Dear Mother, do you think we need to have such fearful anxiety? His friends are as tender with him as anyone could be, and the movement through the balmy air may actually benefit him. At the worst, he won't be more exhausted than he has often been with the old pain. Our not hearing from him by this time is encouraging, I think. We should have heard if anything had gone wrong."

"Don't talk about it!" said Mrs. Holman sharply. "I can never forgive myself, and your father will never forgive me if — "

Margaret quickly interrupted her before the fateful words could be added. "Oh, Mother, shouldn't David's bedclothes be brought in before the dew begins to fall? The sun has left that part of the yard. And I think there should be a little fire started in his room; the evening is going to be chilly."

Frances blessed her for this sudden return to safe, sweet commonplace. How blessed to be able to think of the fresh, sweet-smelling bedclothes being tucked about David and of shading his eyes from the light as usual. Oh, to be sure of going back only to yesterday and having everything just as usual!

The fire was made, the well-aired blankets duly arranged, and everything was sweet and fresh and in waiting; yet no one came. The early dusk began to close them in. Frances drew the shades and lighted the lamps and prepared the rooms for the usual evening as best she could. The mother dropped all attempt at words. She sat with hands clasped in her lap and such a look of misery upon her face, which seemed to have aged since morning, that her daughters turned instinctively from the sight.

In the dining room the table was laid for four. Margaret, as she added the fourth plate, had murmured something about her father being home for supper. As the hours passed, she began to say to Frances in hushed, frightened tones, "If only Father were here!"

"Something dreadful must have happened!" she

said at last, her words sharp with fear. "They certainly wouldn't keep him out after nightfall. Frances, if you had chosen to do so, I believe you could have spared us this day of misery. I hope the realization of it may not embitter your life. Look at Mother! I certainly should not like it for a memory that I might have saved her this."

"Listen!" exclaimed Frances in reply. Hurrying to the door, she strained her eyes to peer into the gathering darkness.

In the near distance voices could be heard shouting — not, apparently, notes of terror or dismay, but certainly sharpened by great excitement. Something had happened! The door was speedily closed, and both girls sought their mother. She, too, had heard the noise. She came out from that empty room and dropped into the chair farthest from the door. She was ready, she believed, for what was to come to her.

"What is it?" she said with a voice that was too quiet. "Why don't you tell me at once what it is? I am ready."

"We don't know, Mother," said Frances, trying to speak cheerily. "There's great excitement on the street, and many people seem to be coming this way. But it can't be anything terrible; they are too noisy. Listen! I can distinctly hear the shouts. Dear Mother, don't look so dreadful! It can't have to do with us in any way. Some political news must have excited the people."

Mrs. Holman made no reply. Margaret clasped her hands in an agony of apprehension — one moment crying out that it was too cruel to keep them in such suspense, and the next trying to assure herself that she feared nothing and that it was silly to get so wrought up. The mother sat with eyes fixed on that outer door, waiting.

The tramp of many feet could now be heard distinctly, though the voices had been hushed. Was this out of respect for the people in that home? A moment more, and the sound of feet was heard on the walk leading to the door. At last somebody was coming! Frances had believed that almost anything would be better than that awful waiting, but she shrank now from all human speech. Yet she must not shrink. She must be strong to meet whatever was coming. She must shield her mother.

This last thought made her leap forward quickly and throw open the door. And she met, not the lifeless form she had schooled herself to expect, nor yet the stretcher that she had watched being borne away in the morning, but instead one who frightened her as mortal had never done before. The face and, above all, the smile were David's own. But he stood on strong feet and seemed the very embodiment of health and strength!

"Have I frightened you?" he asked quickly. "Where is my mother?" He went swiftly toward her chair in time to catch her fainting form in his arms. Mrs. Holman had mistaken her strength; she was ready for the stretcher, but not for this strong man.

Frances — when her strength returned so she could move at all — closed the outer door gently. It came to her that it was almost a pity to shut out that ravishing sight from the eager, sympathizing throng — David, the utterly helpless, standing there straight and strong, holding his mother in his arms!

The crowd waited for a moment or two in respectful silence. Then they gathered their strength for one mighty cheer and tramped away. The family did not know it at the time but discovered afterward that the four young men, who had been David's patient and watchful attendants during that wonderful day, waited, quite outside the gate, even for hours, to see if they might be of service still. To intrude upon that home that night for any other purpose than helpfulness would have seemed to them like sacrilege.

It may have been a merciful Providence that held the three inside that closed door absorbed over their mother. For a time they almost feared that the ancient proverb was mistaken, and joy could kill. Yet was it any wonder that the mother lay as one dead in the arms of her son? Consider what a day it had been, and what years it had followed.

Over and over and *over* again had that poor mother fought her battle with death, when it had seemed to come to claim her boy. She had also fought the battle with her own heart and after many wounds and bruises believed she had submitted to the inevitable. From that time on she had watched the beloved body grow more and more emaciated each day. In her deepening depression she had begun to say, "It can be but a question of months now, instead of years," and had learned to pray that the end might come with as little pain as possible.

Then the strain of that terrible day had come, and the husband on whose judgment she was used to leaning was away and ignorant of all that was transpiring. Certain portions of the day had seemed like years. She had held herself in check so far as any outward sign was concerned, but her imagination had run riot. Every sound on the street meant the footfall of a messenger coming to tell her that out on the noisy street of the city, with no mother near to pillow his dying head, the end had come.

And then the door had opened at last, and she had seen, not her son, but a vision of him, straight, strong, beautiful, as she had known him in his youth! What wonder that the long-controlled powers gave way?

She rallied at last but had nearly fainted again when she saw that it was her son who knelt beside her with one hand feeling for her pulse and the other bathing her forehead. Could she ever get used to being ministered to by him?

When at last they gathered about that belated tea table — oh, the wonder of it! David occupied the extra chair!

"I didn't set the table for you," affirmed Margaret gleefully. "I kept hoping that Father would come to help us get through the night. I felt sure that Mother would need somebody to help her. Who could have imagined that it would ever be you?"

David's eyes sought his mother's face and lingered there.

"You frightened me," he said. "I bemoan my foolishness in not sending a messenger ahead to prepare the way. It's a pity for a man to be so full of himself that he can forget his mother! I didn't realize that the joy of it could overcome you so!"

"It doesn't matter," she said gratefully. "Nothing matters now. I think I shall not mind anything anymore, ever! I am sorry I gave you such a greeting, though. I can't see why I fainted. I have kept up well all day, haven't I, girls? But it was growing so late, and we had not heard a word."

"I know. It was cruel of me. We might have sent

a messenger back to you from time to time if we had thought. But there was nothing to tell. We had to wait. The house was thronged. We were there for hours trying to get near enough even to see the gateway. At one time it seemed as if I'd have to give it up and be brought home in the same way I went. Words will never describe how I felt at the thought! But the crowd was something fearful! Away out into the road and down the road as far as we could see were people, everyone as anxious to get inside the building as I was. Most of them, however, could walk and push for themselves, while I had to be kept where they could not even brush against me.

"The boys were splendid! Not for a single moment did they yield to discouragement. When I forced myself to murmur that perhaps we ought to go back, they said, 'No, indeed! Not for the world will we go back now after the worst has been borne so well.' Dear, blessed fellows! I can never forget what they have been to me this day."

The rush of feeling stopped his voice for a moment, but impetuous Margaret could not wait.

"Go on!" she said eagerly. "How long did you wait, and what happened? Tell us everything. We have done all the waiting that we can this day."

He smiled on her and continued his story: "I have no clear idea how long the wait was. Some of the time I was in very great pain, which made the minutes seem like hours. Then there would come a lull, and I took some rest; I believe I even slept a while. At last, by an ingenious device on the part of my friends, they succeeded in getting me into the place where he was speaking. The effort caused me great agony. They had to push among the people a little, though I was so much worse off than most that they fell back for me and showed some sympathy. But the pain was fearful! I remember that just the moment before my couch was set down in front of him I felt that human nature could endure it no longer. The rest — "

At this point he came to a full stop, as one who felt that he had something to tell for which human language was inadequate. His audience watched him and waited with interest too deep for questions.

CHAPTER IV

WHO HEALETH ALL THY DISEASES

he rest," he said again, with a rare smile on his face, "I wish I could tell it to you! But it is beyond words. I am afraid you will never hear the story. Mother, he used no medicine, asked no questions, spoke not a dozen words. But they were words for *me*; they burned into my soul. Then he added a direction. What do you think? I was to rise and walk!"

Mother and daughters each uttered an exclamation of dismay. They had seen him walk twice across the room. They knew that the impossible had been accomplished. Yet to hear the story from David's own lips and to learn that the result had followed a simple direction seemed beyond belief.

"You must wonder how I dared to try," he began after a moment of silence, "but no sooner had I heard the words than I knew that I could obey them. I felt a strange thrill in these long-unused limbs of mine, a sense of strength and power. Without a second's hesitation, I sprang up before them all and walked. Walked! That is putting it mildly. Mother, I *ran*, like a schoolboy — I jumped! I think I even shouted! I knew then, as well as I do now, that I could walk as far and as fast as any man among them."

Without the living witness before their eyes, how could they have believed such a story? It seemed almost impossible, even while looking at him. Yet there he was, apparently in the full glow of health and strength! Older, he looked, than when he had sat at the family table with them before the terrible accident, but certainly not less vigorous. Also, there was a new look on his face that the ever-watchful mother had never seen there before. A restful, quieting look. It made her feel that here was one who could help shoulder some of her day-to-day cares for her, but she did not understand the change. The youthful David had not been thoughtful of others, and nobody had been able to lean on him.

He had little more to tell. They had the story, he assured them, so far as it could be put into words. The waiting had been long. But the act itself had been accomplished in a moment, and he had moved away and given place to others. The listeners questioned and cross-questioned and could not be satisfied. They went over each detail as though they would never be weary of hearing of it; yet they could not understand.

Suddenly Frances asked the all-important question: "David, how does he explain his extraordinary power? Who is he?"

Her brother turned toward her, a peculiar light on his face and a certain quality in his voice that she could not quite interpret. Yet his words were simple enough.

"I don't know what he claims, Frances. Remember that I never saw him before, and I saw him today only for a moment. I wasn't near enough to hear any words from his lips but those spoken to me. Naturally I did not linger when I found that I could fairly run home! He looks and acts in many respects like other men. At least there is nothing in dress or manner that seems to claim distinction. Yet he is not like others. There is an air of quiet dignity which is forceful and at the same time winning, and he gives one a sense of reserve power. It almost seemed to me that he might be a prophet, such as used to be in the long ago — though I can't imagine any prophet quite like him, and I don't think he has made any such claim. I am compelled to say, therefore, that I do not know who or what he is. I am sure only of this — that whatever he says of himself, I shall believe."

"Of course," said Frances simply. "How could one give less faith than that to a man who evidently lives to bless others and who has a power to do so which is certainly not like other men's?"

Margaret gave her sister a searching look that seemed to be almost a startled one, but she said nothing.

"Well," said David at last, making the first move to leave the table at which they had lingered long, "what is the next thing to be done? Remember that I must be educated again for ordinary, everyday life. My own life has run in unusual grooves for so long that I suppose I have forgotten the routine. This table is to be cleared, is it not, and the dishes cleaned? That used to be the way, I am sure. Dear old dining room! How well I remember it. You were right, Frances, about the bay window. It's better on that side and is surely a great improvement. It looks larger than I had pictured it from the measurements. You have no idea how much I have wished to see the new kitchen. I could never decide just how it was arranged. Let's go and look at it."

He was making an obvious effort to turn the channel of conversation to the safe level of everyday commonplaces for a little while, to relieve the almost terrible strain of excitement under which the mother was struggling.

Margaret caught his idea and helped it along. "The *new* kitchen!" she repeated, as she sprang up to lead the way. "It lost that name long ago. It is nearly three years since it was built!"

A little later, while Margaret and his mother were both away, David sought a word with his elder sister. "I saw Philip today, Frances."

The flush on her face deepened, but she spoke quietly. "Did you? Where was he? I didn't know he had returned."

"He came only yesterday, he said, and had been unusually busy. But he hoped to get out by tomorrow. I saw him there, where the physician was staying. It was he who helped to make a way for me through the crowd. He wasn't surprised to see me, he said. He had felt sure for some days that I would come, and he wasn't surprised at the result."

The young man was watching his sister's face with care while he spoke. As she passed near him in her work of setting the room in order, he put out his hand and drew her to him.

"Am I right, Frances," he said, speaking low, "in imagining that you did not share Mother's and Margaret's feelings about all this? Did you in your secret heart want me to see this wonderful man, and did you almost believe that he could and would help me?"

"Oh, David! I don't know what I thought or what I wanted. I have never seen him, you remember. But we have heard such strange things! And some of them came too directly to be discredited. I couldn't help, sometimes, hoping that — and yet I didn't — ," she stopped abruptly.

"I understand," he said. "You felt what you were almost afraid to think and wanted what you were quite afraid to say. It was very much my own frame of mind. But for my four brave, persistent friends, I couldn't have brought myself to the decision. But, Frances, I thought possibly Philip had told you some things about this man."

"He has," said Frances earnestly. "Oh, he has told me a great deal! But he is young and enthusiastic, and I have been afraid — there is Father, you know."

"I know," David answered. He stifled a rising sigh that seemed to belong to the words and smiled instead as he said, "It seems wonderful that I can sigh over anything tonight. My dear sister, think what a night it is to me!"

"I think of it every minute! I shall be afraid to go to sleep, lest it may be only a dream banished by morning. Only think of you standing here with your arm around me and with me actually leaning on you!"

"It is no dream," he said with bright gravity,

"and will never be dispelled. Not even death can change it. I know, of course, that this glow of physical strength will not last always. My body will grow weak again, and the day will come when it will give out altogether. Let it! I am content."

There was an unmistakable ring of triumph in his voice. Frances watched him closely in silence. She was sure now that there was something about him she did not understand; she waited for his words.

"There is a part to my story that I have not been able to tell as yet," he said. "I think I can tell you; that is, I think you will understand. I received something today that is infinitely more than bodily healing — something that will last as long as eternity. How shall I put it into words?

"You know how it has been with me during the past year? I have tried to pray. Indeed, I may say that I have formed a habit of prayer, and I have believed, or at least hoped, that I was ready for death. But the way was very misty and gloomy. I had nothing close to comfort when I thought of another world. The most I could reach was a sense of calmness in thinking of the inevitable.

"What will you think when I tell you the first words that that wonderful man said to me today? 'Your sins are forgiven!' You may well start and exclaim. I know just how they thrill you. I felt that they had nothing whatever to do with this poor body with its aches and pains, or rather that they reached far beyond the body and earth and time.

"Frances, I felt within me immediately that the words were true — that I was a sinner forgiven, that I loved God with all my soul and that my one desire in life was to obey Him implicitly! I was not in the least prepared for what immediately fol-

lowed. For the moment I had forgotten my body. I
thought only of that man and of my willingness to
do just as he said. I felt simply amazed because the
first thing that he asked me was, not that I should
show to the world what a triumphant death a forgiven sinner could die, but instead I was to arise
and walk! To die seemed so easy, so reasonable. For
the first time in my life I was ready and willing,
while to walk looked like such an impossibility
that it might almost have staggered my faith."

"But it did not?" Frances's face was a study as
she asked her eager question.

"It did not! As I told you, I knew at once that I
could do it. I knew more than that, Frances — that
I could and would obey him in whatever he asked.
I was sure that under his direction I could do anything, and I proved it."

"It is almost too wonderful for belief!" exclaimed Frances. "Yet we know it is true. There can
be no denying this case. Oh, David, have you
thought that even Father must believe in it? The
last part of your story makes me certain that it is all
of God and that He uses this good man, whoever
he is, as His instrument. If God uses him, surely we
may trust him? Even Father will not be able to
deny it."

There was a pleading note in her voice that did
not escape her brother's ear. His face grew suddenly grave, but he answered with decision.

"Certainly we may, Frances, you and I, and we
will. But I want to warn you, dear, not to hope too
much from Father. He has reached the age when it
is hard to accept new ideas, and for certain reasons
he is peculiarly prejudiced against this movement.
Remember how persistently he has closed his ears
to statements that were as well authenticated as

mine can be. I don't hope for encouragement from him.

"But for you and me — I had a few words with Philip today, as to what he had said to you about it, so I know I may speak plainly. There wasn't time for much conversation; he came only a few minutes before I succeeded in getting into the house. There was much buzzing about my ears at the time — that I ought to be taken home at once. Some were sure that the exposure and fatigue would kill me; that I would not even live to reach home. One man thought the law ought to interfere and force them to take me away.

"Philip suddenly spoke out in a voice loud enough to be heard at some distance. 'He's not going home, not until he sees the doctor!' Then he bent over me and spoke low, 'Let no persuasion tempt you to give it up. You will get in soon. A way will open. That you have been willing to come is almost too good for belief. Did Frances persuade you to come?' "

"No!" said poor Frances, with something like a groan. "I didn't. I was too cowardly to do so."

"Yet you did," her brother answered, smiling. "Your silence was so significant that it acted like a tonic. I understood it, dear, better even than you did. I told Philip so. Then I asked him if he had such utter trust in the man that he felt sure he could help me. His reply was impressive. 'When you have seen him, you will wonder that you could have asked such a question.' When he sent a word for you, I told him I would give it if I reached home, and he replied confidently, 'You will get home; and I would give much to be there to see and hear.' Evidently, Frances, he expected the result which followed. Very soon afterward a way was made for me into the physician's presence. I didn't see Philip again, but I want to, to tell him how fully I understand what he meant. After seeing that man as I saw him, not to trust him would be impossible."

Poor Frances could not suppress a little sigh.

"What is to come of it all?" she asked sadly. "If what you say of Father is true — and then there is Philip's father, so different from ours, and yet so prejudiced in the same way. There is nothing but trouble in store for him if — "

"What are you two talking about?" interrupted Margaret's eager voice, as she appeared from the kitchen. "Mother, Frances is getting something we haven't heard, and that isn't fair, is it? You must just go over everything you have said, David. We are not to miss one word."

"We are not to hear one more word tonight," said David, crossing the room to meet his mother and passing his arm about her in a way that he used to as a boy. "This dear mother has borne all that she can today; she ought to be sleeping."

"I suppose I shall sleep again sometime," said Mrs. Holman, smiling, "but it does not seem now as if I ever could. I'm not tired — joy has rested me." Yet she leaned on her tall son just for the joy of leaning. "I thought of waiting up for your father," she added. "I think he must certainly come tonight, and it will soon be time to expect him."

"Then I will wait up for him with great delight." He laughed at her startled look. "Why not, Mother? I am perfectly well, you know. It wouldn't be possible for a body to feel more thoroughly sound and strong than mine."

She laughed aloud with delight. What joy it was to hear such words from her David's lips! What would his father say? But she made haste to protest.

"Indeed, dear boy, you must go at once to your room. I can lie awake and wait for Father as well as not. And don't you think that we ought to keep this blessed news from him tonight? He is not as young as he used to be, you know, and he won't sleep any tonight, I am sure, if he hears of it."

CHAPTER V

HE HATH PUT A NEW SONG IN MY MOUTH

ou are right," said David promptly. "We must think of my father. Then, Mother, may we kneel down together and thank God for His power and grace?"

The crowning astonishment of the day lay in those words. David Holman on his knees! His mother had not seen him there since he was a mere boy. As a household they gathered morning and evening for prayer. But in those few years of young manhood, before David was laid helpless on his bed, he had been habitually out too late at night and up too late in the morning to join them in outward form. As for heart-worship, if he had ever honestly prayed, his mother thought it must have

52

been in his lisping childhood.

Of late she had shared with Frances the trembling hope that David was changed, that he was at least overcoming the bitter, rebellious spirit that had held him in bondage for many months after his accident and was learning to look to God for mercy. But, in addition to his unwillingness to talk on such topics, her own timidity, aided by long habit, made it almost impossible to gain his confidence. She had spoken nervously once or twice and had found a shred of hope on which to rest her anxious heart. At times she allowed herself to believe that David prayed in secret. But she had never even thought of hoping to hear words of prayer from his lips. Her astonishment, then, over his words can be better imagined than described.

He smiled brightly in response to it. "You didn't think I knew how to pray, did you? I'm not at all sure that I do, in words other than God can understand. But I know that my heart is too full of joy and gratitude tonight not to try. So if you will all kneel with me I will attempt to voice my thought."

The first tears his mother had shed since he left her that morning rolled down her cheeks as she heard her son pour out his gratitude to God for the wonders which had been wrought that day. Even then she did not understand. To her the miracle of the day was the healing of the broken body. But the happy Frances felt that the first words the great doctor spoke to him had been the ones which had thrilled the soul of her brother into life.

"What a blessing it is that we don't have neighbors close by!" Margaret began, as soon as she and Frances were in their room together. "This afternoon, when we were enduring the tortures of waiting, I thought what a relief it would be if only

somebody lived near enough to run in and help
Mother, simply by being here. But tonight I am
glad we are isolated. If we were nearer town, the
house would be crowded with curiosity seekers."

"Or sympathizing friends," Frances reminded
her.

"Well, as to that, the best kind of sympathy, I
think, is to leave us alone until we get used to ourselves. But they won't. Tomorrow the house will be
crowded! People who don't care two straws for us
will come out to see how we act under such strange
conditions. I dread it. I'm sure I don't know how to
act. We are used to receiving people by ourselves
and saying, 'He is not quite so well today,' or 'We
think he is a little easier today than usual, thank
you.' I know all the formulas for that. But to have a
brother who may go to the door when the bell
rings or who will sit in the parlor and visit with the
callers is bewildering. Then think of Father! Oh,
Frances! What will Father say?"

"What can he say, dear, but that a wonderful joy
and blessing have come to his home while he was
away?"

"I know, of course; but, then, I also know Father.
Think how emphatic he has been in his orders to
have nothing to do with this strange man or his
followers. He hadn't a particle of faith in any of the
stories we heard. I think he hates the whole thing."

Frances shivered. "Oh, no! Don't use such a
word in that connection. Father didn't understand
it, and neither do we. But surely no one will hate
what has somehow given us our brother back from
the grave. Father will look upon everything in a
different light after he has seen David. Let's not
talk about it anymore tonight, Margaret. It's very
late, and for David's sake we ought to get quiet as

soon as possible."

This reason, which had been a potent one in the household for years, subdued Margaret's voice but did not prevent her reply. "Call it what you please. But unless I am wonderfully mistaken, Father will act very much as though the word to describe his feelings ought to be 'hate.' He doesn't give up old ideas readily. He couldn't if a miracle were performed before his eyes, and I don't think we have any right to call this a miracle. It is wonderful, of course, and nobody can be more glad over it than I. Still, I must say I dread all the talk and fuss there will be. It won't end in talk — you see if it does. There will be real trouble. If Philip is as much interested in the new doctor as they say he is, you will have reason to dread it, too."

Frances, who had resolved to talk no more, made no attempt at reply. She would not have liked to admit how like lead the foreboding words of her sister sunk into her heart; she had no words to speak to overthrow them.

With only silence left for Margaret, the little house at last grew quiet. As to the amount of sleep that visited its inmates, that is another matter.

David Holman lay quite still in the very corner where he had lain for years. But he was so brimful of the fact that he could turn himself from side to side, rise on his elbow and look about him in the moonlight, yes, even spring out on the floor and walk — run, if he would — that the pure delight of it kept him awake. How could he be expected to accustom himself at once to such a marvelous state of things? Here was the same body which, only that morning, was so tortured with pain that the perspiration almost started anew at the thought of the agony he endured during that long, slow jour-

ney down the road. In imagination he could feel
again the throbs of pain as the eager crowd
brushed by his cot on their way to join the greater
crowds about the door. Yet here was that same
body not only without a sense of ache or pain but
alive to its fingertips with strength and power!

Once he laughed aloud. "I would like to shout
'Hallelujah!' so loud they could hear me down-
town, but I mustn't. I must be very still and let the
others sleep. Tomorrow is coming. How will it feel
to awaken and toss myself about like this?" He
tossed to the other side of the bed and back and
laughed again.

"I'm like a child with a new toy!" he said.
"Think of getting up and dressing myself, as I used
to do! And going out to breakfast and moving
about where I please and being as I used to be! No,
not that part, thank God. Never again as I used to
be. Oh, God, I thank You that I am a new creature
indeed, body and soul!"

He lay awake well into the midnight and was
rewarded at last by the steady march of feet down
the road. He recognized his father's step. Long listening to sounds from the outer world, as a means
of passing the time, had made him skillful. Sometime before the door was reached he was sure that
his father was coming. He lay there longing to
dress and go out and take long strides down the
moonlit road and meet him, but he mustn't. His
mother had been quite right. Joy might not kill, but
his father's hair was very gray, and his step was
feebler than it used to be. The son knew that part of
this was because of him. He was in haste to atone.
He wanted to close his arms about his father's neck
and say, "Father, I am sorry for all the past. Forgive
it, and let me begin all over again. I am a new crea-

ture, and the years to come shall show you how a
new creature can live." But for all this he must wait
until morning.

He counted the footsteps as they sounded at last
on the graveled path and made weary progress toward the door. How plainly they showed that his
father was tired! He heard his mother's voice as
she said, "You are very late!" and his father's response, followed by a question which was always
the same after ever so brief an absence: "How is
David?"

"David is well," said his mother. They had fallen
into this phraseology during these later months of
comparative freedom from pain. It was the shorter
way of saying, "He is as well as can be expected; as
well as you may hope to find him, ever."

It was thus that the father understood the words
at this time, though the listening David laughed
softly as he detected the undertone of joy in his
mother's voice. It was almost a wonder that his
father had not noticed it, but he was very tired. He
did not want anything to eat, he said; he was too
tired for eating. Yes, he had had a weary trip and in
some respects a discouraging one; he was getting
too old for such business. There were details that
needed a younger, quicker brain than his, and he
sighed as he said so; he felt sure that no younger
brain would come to his rescue. And the listener
laughed again a tender, sympathetic laugh.

That watched-for morning came at last and was
fully as exciting as Margaret had imagined. The
father was the first thought, and each member of
the family had planned how best to break the wonderful news to him. Yet, as a matter of fact, the
program was arranged without their help.

Neither of the elder Holmans had slept much,

each trying to keep from waking the other. Mr.
Holman was so exhausted from his trip that he lay
awake for hours. Mrs. Holman, who had believed
she could not close her eyes with all the excitement,
really had not slept until the day dawned. She was
in such a deep sleep when her husband awoke that
he went about on tiptoe and resolved not to dis-
turb her. He was often the first to open David's
door cautiously in the early morning and, if he
proved to be awake, greet him with some question
intended to call out how the night had served him.

Since their invalid had been free enough from
pain to sleep part of the night in relative quiet, they
had arranged for his comfort that he should be left
quite alone. Bells connected to his father's and his
sisters' rooms enabled him to summon whomever
he would at any moment. If he was wakeful and
restless, he was anxious to let one of them come
and share his weariness with him. When neither
bell rang, the family knew that the latter part of the
night had been fairly comfortable.

Very softly indeed was the door pushed open
this morning, lest a possible nap might be disturbed. But David's eyes were wide open, and his
smile was good to see. His face spoke such an unmistakable language that the father omitted the
usual question and hastened forward to greet him,
saying only, "I am glad to see you so comfortable."

Then he stopped midway, staring like one transfixed by fright — for David was sitting upright in
the bed, and his long unused arms were out-
stretched toward his father!

"Don't be afraid of me," he reassured him with a
cheerful laugh. "My dear father, I have been too
sudden, after all, though I have waited all night for
this moment. Let me help you." He sprang from

the bed and threw his strong arms about the trembling form of his father as he almost fell down. "See, I'm dressed and ready for the day. But I lay down again for fear that finding me on my feet might be too sudden a shock for you. And then I was so careless! Sit down, Father, and let me tell you my wonderful story."

He drew up the large armchair that his father usually occupied when he came to read to him. Placing him in it, he threw wide the window to give him air and brought him a glass of water from the pitcher always left for him. They had changed places; the son was ministering to the father. With his head all but leaning on his son's shoulder the father first heard David's story. After the first exclamations of dismay and astonishment, he listened in utter silence.

Even before the whole family had greeted their newly recovered member, the callers Margaret had foreseen began to arrive. The first were David's four friends, who had played so conspicuous a part in the history of the eventful day. They came directly to his room.

"I could not sleep last night for thinking of you," said one, as he clasped the hand of the man who stood erect and at his ease, though still surrounded by all sorts of comforts contrived for one who could not stand at all.

David laughed genially. "I'm not surprised at that, my friend," he said, returning the handclasp with energy. "I couldn't sleep myself. I was so enraptured with the fact that I could toss about on that good old bed of mine which has held me motionless for so long. I found that contrivance for my shoulders in its accustomed place last night. My sister Margaret had carefully arranged it for me. I took it out tenderly and carried it over there, where my eyes could rest on it the first thing in the morning. Boys," his voice growing suddenly tremulous, "you don't know anything about it and never can."

They clasped hands in silence, all of them too much moved for further words.

Breakfast was not yet over when other callers were announced. Before that memorable day was done it seemed to the family that the entire city must have been out to visit them. People who knew them ever so slightly, and people who did not know them at all, came continuously. They often could not frame any excuse for coming, except that of overpowering curiosity to look with their own eyes upon the man of whom they had long heard as helpless and hopeless and convince themselves that he was actually on his feet.

Throughout the exciting day David proved himself the strong one. He met all his visitors graciously, assuring those who tried to apologize for the intrusion that nothing could be more natural and reasonable than their desire to see him face-to-face. He answered innumerable questions heartily and as fully as his own knowledge would allow. In short, he won many accolades all day long, not only from the relieved family, who found the burden of exclusive entertainment thus lifted from their shoulders, but from strangers as well.

The early evening brought a caller who, though entirely unknown to David, was evidently no stranger to his sister Margaret. His keen eyes noted the unusual color on Margaret's cheek as she made the introductions.

"Mr. Masters, I am glad to make you acquainted with my brother, David, of whom you have so often heard."

CHAPTER VI

THEY OPENED THEIR MOUTH WIDE AGAINST ME, AND SAID, 'AHA, AHA, OUR EYE HATH SEEN IT'

asters, repeated David to himself, trying to recall what Frances had told him of this acquaintance. It had been her habit to amuse her brother by very careful descriptions of persons and things connected with the world from which he was shut away. She was very skilled at description and at imitation. David had an amused feeling that he knew several of the people who had called that day, simply from her delineations. But she must have passed Mr. Masters in almost silence. David could remember his name being mentioned once, but that was all.

It could not be that she had considered him too commonplace to demand attention. He was a tall, well-built man, with the regularity of features that belong to the term "fine-looking." He was also exceedingly well dressed, with a careful regard to small details that marked him as a man well up in the customs of polite society. This David felt, rather than knew, because very few of his callers were from the class known as society people.

The eyes held his attention. He could not be quite sure what they said. They fascinated him by their brilliance, but — did they at the same time slightly repel him? He was sure that they knew how to flash sharply on occasion, and it was very evident that they knew how to smile for Margaret. The two dropped naturally into talk that seemed to interest them both.

David, saying little, continued his mental studies. Masters — I wonder if he is connected with the governor's family. Can Margaret really be interested in him? Surely not or Frances would have told me. I don't think my father would like that, not if — . His mental queries were cut short by the arrival of another caller. This time it was Philip Nelson.

David sprang to meet him, and the two stood silently apart from the others with clasped hands for some seconds — both so nearly overcome by a rush of memories as to be beyond speech.

Mr. Masters watched them with an interested, but was it also a slightly cynical, smile?

"Your brother has discovered a friend," he said to Margaret.

"Oh, yes," agreed Margaret. "That is a discovery that was made years ago. David has always been close to Philip Nelson."

"Has he indeed!" said Mr. Masters. "Do you know I am somewhat surprised? There is a striking contrast between the two men, entirely in favor of your brother. However, I suppose people shut away from society often form friendships merely on the basis of propinquity. I can imagine your brother becoming strongly attached to persons who were thoughtful of him during his exile."

Frances Holman, who had just been to the hall with departing callers, stood near enough to hear these words. She turned grave, questioning eyes on the speaker's face and said in very distinct tones, "One would almost imagine from your tone, Mr. Masters, that you could, if you chose, bring serious charges against the gentleman of whom you are speaking. May I ask if you know any reason why he should not be my brother's intimate friend?"

Mr. Masters laughed lightly. "Indeed not, Miss Holman. I would not for the world convey such an impression. I was only intimating to your sister that I had formed a higher estimate of your brother's mental calibre than such a friendship suggested. But I have only the very slightest acquaintance with your friend Mr. Nelson and therefore should not presume to judge."

He turned at once to another topic, his manner indicating that he considered that one too trivial to hold his attention further. But Frances's expressive face showed her disturbance.

Nothing had been actually said against Philip Nelson. But the tone and manner of Margaret's aristocratic friend had certainly been offensive, and there had been a flash in his eyes that she did not like. She studied the incident anxiously. Perhaps this young man, who stood high in political as well as social circles, was Philip's enemy.

These were troubled times in more than one direction, and Philip's way, for reasons that she understood better than most, was already hedged in by difficulties. She wished she had not spoken to Mr. Masters. What sudden temptation had prompted her? She was not given to calling people to account for apparently trivial expressions of opinion. Perhaps she had prejudiced Mr. Masters more fully than he had been before. He was the sort of man, she thought, to remember disagreeably a word like hers. Suddenly she became aware that the crowded little parlor was giving undivided attention to Philip Nelson and that he was eagerly attempting to describe the personal appearance of the stranger-physician and teacher who was exciting such general interest.

"You seem to be quite familiar with this extraordinary person, Mr. Nelson." This was the statement which suddenly interrupted the eager flow of words. It was Felix Masters who spoke.

Frances, as she marked the inflection which she could not help thinking covered a sneer, wondered how Margaret could admire that man.

Philip turned toward him as one surprised at being interrupted, but he answered quietly, "I am somewhat acquainted with him, sir. At least I have met him several times."

"You are a friend of his, perhaps?"

The questioner's manner was certainly growing markedly offensive. If he had thought to embarrass Philip Nelson, he was disappointed.

That young man's voice was never clearer than when he replied, "I count myself honored in being able to claim him as a friend."

"I am very sorry to hear it." The slow, deliberate voice of the elder Mr. Holman spoke these words. Up to that point he had taken no part in the conversation. But when Philip Nelson began to speak, an observer would have seen that the host had leaned forward with ears attentive to catch every word. The face of his daughter Frances flushed, and she picked nervously at a flower that someone in passing had laid in her lap. Philip turned a look not so much of surprise as of inquiry upon the speaker and waited respectfully.

Mr. Holman evidently felt that the time had come for him to speak. He cleared his throat and, still speaking very slowly, as if he were weighing each word, said, "In my judgment, and I have given the matter careful thought, as you may well suppose, that person who has come among us so suddenly and who is conducting himself so strangely, is a dangerous character. I think the future will prove this to be the case. And I think that the less you young men have to do with him in any way, the better it will be for you and for your friends."

"Amen!" said Felix Masters with great promptness and alacrity.

Philip, evidently relieved, addressed the inquiry he was about to make to the younger man. "Why do you think so, sir? What do you know of him that suggests a dangerous character? Has he thus far done anything but good in the towns where he has visited?"

Mr. Masters gave a slight, contemptuous laugh, before he said, "Oh, I have no fault to find with what he has *done*, so far as it goes. There is certainly no harm in leading a few simple-minded or hypochondriac old men and women to understand that they are well enough, if they only think so. Of course there is nothing new or strange about that. Since the world began there have been those who, for a consideration, were prepared to make the lame walk and the nervous imagine themselves well or sick, whichever best suited the purpose of the performer."

"Since the world began have many such cases as this one come under your observation?" As he spoke, Philip Nelson laid his hand on the arm of his friend David.

Mr. Masters laughed again, that light, peculiar, offensive laugh, as he said, "I do not know that I am prepared for a cross-examination. I hadn't expected to be placed on trial this evening, so I haven't the evidence ready. Neither, by the way, am I a physician. But I have a friend who is, whose opinion might be interesting to you. He makes no marvel even of such cases as our friend Mr. Holman's. He says there are instances on record that prove the remarkable influence the mind has over matter, when the right moment comes for rousing the latter to action.

"I have no doubt myself but that the present instance, which you are tempted to ascribe to the miraculous, can be explained on an entirely reasonable basis. Probably the disease which has so long prostrated Mr. Holman was stayed long ago. We must remember that he has been the subject of the most skillful medical treatment that could be found in this country, and during his long, quiet rest, nature has been reasserting her claims and has without noise or tumult performed a really wonderful cure. The truth is, the old Dame is constantly doing wonders for us, which we, with bad taste and doubtful honesty, are always ready to attribute to some physician.

"Mind you, I am entirely ready to admit that our friend Mr. Holman had no knowledge of the cure;

that, too, is natural. Since he was long accustomed to inactivity from necessity, he grew into the belief that the necessity was upon him as a fixed law. In obedience to a strong-willed person in the full vigor of all his physical powers, he was moved by the subtle law of personal magnetism — which I also admit that we by no means fully understand — to do for himself that which simply proved his cure. Immediately the credulous world is agog with cries of 'a miracle!' while the fact is that nothing is simpler to students of science than such natural results from the use of natural laws."

Frances Holman's face, from being deeply flushed, had grown very pale. Her eyes glanced nervously from Philip Nelson to her father, then back again to Philip. She felt herself on the verge of a moral earthquake. Undoubtedly Philip would make some reply to this harangue which would help to bring it all about. The strain upon her nerves was unexpectedly interrupted by a laugh — not a mocking one, simply a joyous outburst from David Holman. Without the addition of a word, it seemed almost able to overturn the remarkable bit of logic to which they had just been treated.

But David's voice followed the laugh. "My good friend, there is only one way in life, so far as I know, to convince you of the utter fallacy of your argument. That would be to set you down in the place that I occupied only yesterday morning and let you suffer what I did in being moved and carried by ever so gentle hands through the streets. The experience would have convinced you in less than three minutes that something beyond nature was needed to subdue the demon of pain that for every step of the way and for five terrible hours afterward had me in possession. God forbid, however, that you should ever have to learn through the medium of such a teacher!" His voice grew solemn as he proceeded, and a shiver ran through his frame, as though the memory of the suffering was a furnace to him.

But Mr. Masters was apparently unmoved. "A psychological discussion carried on extempore!" he said lightly, as he arose to depart. "The ladies must excuse us for forcing such abstruse and possibly unpleasant themes upon them, and I, at least, must cut the important discussion short by retiring. It is later than I had supposed."

"But, Masters," interrupted a young man who, although he had been a very attentive listener, had up to that moment been silent, "before you go I wish you would explain one remark of yours. What do you mean by calling that man a dangerous person? It surely cannot be dangerous, as you hinted yourself, to set people on their feet again, even though we grant that their illness may have been only imaginary. He does them good service by so much, at least, and nobody has explained wherein the harm lies."

"The harm, my friend, lies, as I imagine that thoughtful people older than you have discovered" — with a slight graceful bow toward the elder Mr. Holman — "in getting hold of the masses by devices of this character and leading them to think that some mysterious power works through him. Then, when the moment is ripe for action, he leads them whither he will, in ways that they have not imagined. In short, since you almost force frankness from me, I will say that I believe the man to be a political intriguer, in league with the enemies of our country. I am not speaking carelessly on such a subject, as you may well suppose. I have access to knowledge of importance that makes me somewhat confident of what I affirm, and I consider the warning of our friend Mr. Holman most timely and of very great importance."

With another bow for Mr. Holman, and with the air of a sage who had fulfilled his duty toward the rising generation, this wise young man of twenty-five took his leave. The other callers followed his example, stopping for only a few words of general and desultory conversation. Mr. Nelson was the last to say good night, and David arose as he did, remarking that the evening was so lovely that he envied his walk to town. Then he summoned Frances to a walk on the piazza, and the three left together.

As soon as they were beyond other ears, Philip Nelson turned toward his friend.

"Thank you for your brave words tonight, David. I supposed that I was to take the defensive quite alone."

"But for my father's sake," said David quickly, "I should have spoken much more plainly than I did. It seems due to my father that my first explanation or expression of opinion should be given to him."

Frances looked from one grave face to the other, with an interest not unmingled with anxiety.

"I don't think I understand," she said. "Why should your words be spoken of as brave? Why shouldn't one be outspoken in one's gratitude, at least? And what more is there that can be said?"

Philip waited for the brother to speak; but as David remained silent, he turned to Frances. "You heard what Felix Masters said tonight? He considers David's benefactor a dangerous person, a man who is trying to raise a following that will stir up treason. Such words, coming from such a source, are full of meaning. There are those who, for reasons best understood by them, will hail all such expressions and do what they can to foster and develop them in due time. I may be mistaken; I hope I am. But I feel in my soul that the time is coming, is not far distant, when to speak even such words in our teacher's favor, as we did tonight, will require courage of no mild type."

" 'Our teacher'! Are you then one of his pupils, Philip?"

The young man held out his hand to her with a grave smile, as he said, "I am indeed, my friend. It won't be possible for long to keep the matter secret, and certainly I have no desire to do so. I am glad to own it. I would have told you before this, had there been an opportunity. But there were reasons why it seemed wise not to speak plainly everywhere. Still, I don't think it comes to you as a surprise, does it?"

"No," said Frances in a low, trembling voice. She could not trust herself to add another word.

"Good night," said Philip abruptly, giving the hand that he held an earnest pressure. "I mustn't say more now, though I want to. I hope, by the time I see you again, that matters will have so shaped themselves as to justify me in speaking what my heart prompts. Until then, trust me."

CHAPTER VII

I Will Not Refrain My Mouth

They watched him taking rapid strides down the road, they two, pacing silently up and down the moonlit space.

Frances felt that when she spoke again it must be about something that had nothing to do with Philip Nelson.

"How wonderful it is," she said presently, "that I am taking a walk on the piazza with you!"

But David could not get away from the recent train of thought. "And how wonderful it is," he said soberly, "that the one who made such an experience possible seems to have few friends to speak for him and is even sneered at in my father's house as a 'dangerous person'!"

And then Frances's mood suddenly changed, and she felt that she could talk about nothing else but the thought which oppressed her. "David, do you really think there is any danger to be feared for those who call themselves his followers?"

"Not actual danger, perhaps, but disagreeable notoriety and the rending of some friendships."

Frances shivered, but it was not with cold; and her brother, as he passed a protecting arm around her, knew that it was not.

"Poor Philip!" he said. "Do you know that I think he's been passing through a temptation. The way would have been so much easier for him if he could have kept silent with regard to this matter. He can't help foreseeing what effect his speaking out may have upon our father. Yet it wasn't possible, of course, to keep to such a line of conduct. One cannot stand on neutral ground concerning that man. The fact is, people who come in contact with him must decide to be either for or against him. You see, don't you, that Philip could not have done other than he has?"

"I certainly would not want anyone to act contrary to his convictions of right for the sake of my friendship," was her somewhat tremulous reply.

"Certainly you wouldn't. Be sure that Philip understands you. By the way, Frances, how much or how little does that man Masters mean? There can't be any real friendship between him and Margaret, can there? I tried to recall what you had said to me about him, but I find that my thoughts are very vague."

"I haven't said much about him, not since the first call, because I haven't known what to say. I haven't the least idea how serious his intentions are, but I know that I distrust him. It has troubled me, David, that intimacy. And the only reason I have not spoken is because I thought I mustn't trouble you. I don't know that I have good reason for distrusting him, but I can't help the feeling. He is showing what in some men would be called marked attention to Margaret, and I'm afraid she is interested in him."

"Do you know if he is connected with the governor's family?"

"Oh, yes, the governor is his uncle, as he is inclined to let one know on every possible occasion. I'm surprised the fact did not appear this evening. Someone said one evening in talking over a local matter, 'I wonder what position Governor Masters takes?' And the young man answered promptly, 'Why, my uncle....' Oh, he stands at the very head of what they call society. I suppose there isn't a young lady in town who wouldn't feel flattered to be the object of such attentions as he has shown to Margaret. But I wish she had never seen him."

"I appreciate your feeling," her brother sighed slightly. "Little as I have seen of the gentleman, I could find it in my heart to echo your wish."

A summons from the parlor interrupted further talk. It was the hour for family prayer. Mr. Holman looked worn. The habitual gravity, not to mention sternness of his face — the lines of which had been softened earlier in the day by the sudden joy that had come to his home — seemed to have returned. In his prayer he by no means forgot to thank God fervently for sending renewed health and vigor to the body so long deprived of them. But in almost the same breath he prayed that they might all be kept from drawing hasty conclusions or being led into error by false teachers who were able to appear as "angels of light." David and Frances, as they arose from their knees, exchanged sad smiles that were full of meaning.

Mr. Ezra Holman's character, in order to be understood, must be more carefully explained. He was a good man, in the accepted meaning of that phrase — a man whose word was to be trusted as fully as his oath could have been; a man whose affection for his family was strong and steady and never showed in words or caresses. He was strictly just, or meant to be, but rarely merciful in the true sense. He stood so rigorously for what he believed to be right that he let it tempt him sometimes into severe ways of maintaining the right. Take notice that the sentence reads: "He stood for what he *believed* to be right," which is often a very different thing from the right. He lived, in short, confined between narrow grooves. An act was right because it was *right*, and it was wrong because it was *wrong*. And the people were "shallow" or "frivolous" or "dishonest" who disagreed with him. Such, in brief, were his forms of logic.

What had once been the accepted explanation of a fact must be adhered to tenaciously in the face of all modern proof that the idea was an error. The very antiquity of the belief seemed in some way to enhance its importance in his eyes. Such a man had, of course, his own ideas concerning the development of the human race and the intentions of God with regard to it. To move outside of the regular channel, which he did not in the least realize that he had helped to dig, was little short of blasphemy.

This being the case, it will be understood that the manner of his son's cure was a shock to him. It was entirely outside of that channel. In truth, this father, with tears in his eyes and a great ache in his

heart but with great positiveness of belief had settled it long ago that the Lord did not intend his son
ever to walk the earth again. This was to be his just
retribution for transgressing the laws of health.
Therefore, for any person to interfere with the
Lord's plans and effect a cure — would it be almost
a sin?

No, the poor father did not actually mean that,
not consciously at least. He had been held in the
arms of that recovered son and had shed tears of
joy over the marvel. He could not quite forget that.
But two hours after the experience he had set to
work to construct a theory of the cure that would
run in the aforesaid channel. That it was to be cred-
ited to the power of the dangerous man, whose
views and teaching he believed he had looked into
sufficiently to discover them to be false and dangerous in the extreme, was not to be thought of for
a moment. How, then, should the almost miracle
be explained?

To one who understood the young man's condition as well as his father did, it was certainly a
difficult task. The day had been full of unrest and
perplexity. But the coming of that brilliant scientist
and logician, Felix Masters, had brought a flood of
light. Listening to his explanation, the truth had
flashed upon the father so fully that he wondered
at his dullness in not understanding it before.

David had been steadily improving for years;
they all knew that. The days when he needed constant watching and when every hour was fraught
with danger of the end had long gone by. Nothing
was more reasonable than that the improvement
had been much greater than they or he realized. Of
course, he had not tried to move himself. Why
should he, when he believed it to be impossible?

What had been needed was a sudden shock that would send the blood tingling through those long-unused limbs. Such a shock the unusual effort and excitement, followed by the long journey over rough streets, had produced; hence the result. There was no more miracle about it than there is about any violent action of the laws of nature.

The explanation Mr. Masters gave was certainly entirely satisfying to any reasonable mind. It would be difficult to put into language an idea of the sense of relief the poor man felt when that disturbed channel was again in order.

Yet there were perplexities still. Was it an instinct or a premonition of trouble that made him feel that neither David nor his daughter Frances, which was in some respects a sorer trial, accepted the logic so satisfactory to him? That the son of the house should have extravagant ideas and headstrong ways of his own was in a sense to be expected. It had been the manner of sons as far back as he could remember, and David had too sadly proved already that he was in that direction keeping up with tradition. But Mr. Holman was a man who believed there was not even in nature any excuse for daughters going astray. It was a slight relief to remember that if his eldest daughter failed him, the blame could be laid at Philip Nelson's door. But still, the perplexed and wearied old man saw trouble ahead and longed for peace — and was unhappy.

Several days passed, however, in comparative quiet. People still came in great numbers to call, and David took upon himself almost entirely the duty of entertaining them. Between times he took long walks over the hills, occasionally with Frances for a companion, but as a rule quite alone.

He was busy with certain problems that needed thought, but he came and went with a cheerful face and was undoubtedly enjoying perfect soundness of body.

He knew that his mother was haunted with an unspoken fear that the strength which had so suddenly and, she felt, marvelously — despite all the logic she had heard — returned to him would as suddenly leave him. He saw the fear in her eyes as she looked up quickly to welcome his return. He always had a reassuring smile for her and an immediate evidence of his continued strength.

It was after one of these long walks that what may perhaps be called another crisis in this young man's life came to him.

He had taken a seat near his mother and helped himself to her spool and scissors to toy with while he talked. It was an old habit of his that the mother remembered well. Indeed, it had been one of those little memories that had more than once started bitter tears over the thought that such happy carelessness would never be again.

"I've been up on Watch Hill," he said.

"Not away up!" the mother exclaimed with satisfaction. Only happy mothers of sons can understand how happy it made her to have her David sit there and snip a very useful piece of cloth into useless bits. "Wasn't that a long walk for such a warm afternoon?"

"It is rather warm, but I enjoyed the walk. I had no thought of getting tired. Yes, I went quite to the top. The view there is what it always was. But, after all, the view below was the grand one. Mother, have you heard that Michael is at home again?"

"Not Michael!" His mother dropped her work in

her lap and looked not only surprised but dismayed. "You don't mean it, David! What in the world can they do with him? I thought he was to be taken care of at the hospital as long as he lived?"

"That was the plan, but it has been frustrated. Instead, he has come home to take care of his mother and sister. They don't keep well people in the hospitals, you know, Mother. He was hoeing the garden like a man who felt that he had much lost time to make up."

Mrs. Holman resumed her sewing. "Who are you talking about, David? For the moment, I thought you meant Michael Payne."

"So I do. An incurable disease he had, you know, in its worst form. I remember saying, and hearing others say, when he was sent to the hospital that in his old home it was the same as death. But see how mistaken we were! He is not only at home again but at work vigorously and is in splendid health."

The look of bewilderment on Mrs. Holman's face was deepening every moment.

"David!" she said, startled. "How can that be true? I saw Michael once after he went to the hospital, and the sight was so terrible that I could never forget it. I begged his mother not to go anymore. You must have mistaken someone else for poor Michael; it is so long since you have seen him. Oh, I understand it — you saw his brother Joe. They say he looks very much as Michael used to."

"My dear mother, do you believe I could have let myself be deceived after my own so recent experience? It was Michael Payne himself; I'd know him anywhere. Besides, I had a long talk with him and heard his story. It simply means that the same man who spoke the word of power to me met him one day and sent him home to his mother — cured."

A look of solemn joy rested on David's face. His mother had seen it there before and wondered over it. There was much about this son of hers in these days that she did not understand, but there had been nothing to give her pain.

Before she could reply to the astounding bit of news he had given her, Mr. Holman, who was sitting at his desk presumably busy among his papers, wheeled his chair around and spoke with more than his habitual dignity. "David, I wish you would not use that sort of jargon; it is very offensive. You know, of course, that I don't believe in any such power as you have hinted at, and it is painful for me to hear such hints from a son of mine. I've been intending to speak plainly to you. I want you to remember in time and not mix up your family in any way with the people who are running wild after this adventurer."

Mrs. Holman looked very anxious, but David's voice was calm and controlled.

"I would be sorry, indeed, Father, to seem to lack respect for you. I hope you won't view it in that light. I'm more sorry than I can express to have to hold different views from you. But after what I have experienced, I would despise myself if I kept silent. If it seems to be 'jargon' to you to speak in honor of the one who gave me back my life in a moment of time, I am bitterly sorry. But when I have the opportunity, I must speak."

The father moved restlessly in his chair, making an obvious effort to hold himself in check and speak calmly. "It is certainly natural, perhaps, that you would attach more importance to the man's influence than common sense would dictate. In your weak bodily condition, you were, of course, an easy victim to fanaticism. That's why I've waited patiently for your good sense to come to your rescue. You were not easily deceived, even when you were much younger than you are now — not in these lines, at least. What can the man be but an imposter, making skillful use of his knowledge of mental conditions and of the power of mind over matter? That young man's explanation the other night ought to satisfy any reasonable person. In your case, nature had, as he said, effected a cure, and none of us had discovered it. But, of course, we should have done so soon. I regret deeply that I was not at home to prevent your falling into the hands of one who was ready to take advantage of the weakness of your body to get control of your mind."

CHAPTER VIII

WHO HATH BELIEVED OUR REPORT?

avid opened his lips to speak, but his mother interposed eagerly. "Father, you couldn't have heard what David was telling me. He says that Michael Payne is at home again and is perfectly well."

"Stuff and nonsense!" was the father's irritable response. "Don't, Hannah, try to support your children in false and foolish notions that will ruin us all! We don't want to join the rabble who are making mountains out of molehills. Our family has ranked among the respectable for generations. I hope our branch will not disgrace the name. You all act as though something very new had happened. A love of the marvelous is born with some people, but I never supposed that my family was of that class.

"Haven't people ever been known to have serious diseases and to recover from them by natural processes? I myself have known cases so bad as to be mistaken for incurable disease, but time and nature cured them for all that.

"It is high time we had done with such folly as this. I will have no more of it in my house, and I want you all to understand it. I tell you it is worse than jargon; it is sheer blasphemy! I want you all to keep away from those people and their ideas. Look at the set that their so-called leader has gathered about him! Who are they? Ignorant fellows who are discontented with their sphere in life — too lazy to work and ready for the first excitement that comes along."

His own excitement seemed to increase with every word he said; he had raised his voice almost to a shout. David, noting this, had changed his mind and decided on perfect silence. But Margaret, who had been drawn from the next room by the sound of her father's voice, seemed unable to resist the temptation to speak. Whether her motive had a touch of maliciousness in it or whether she honestly believed the reminder would calm her father's indignation, David could not be sure.

"Why, Father," she said, "you have forgotten Philip. Didn't you hear him declare himself honored to call that man his friend? He is respectable certainly."

"He is in no sense remarkable," said Mr. Holman, his voice not as loud, but his irritation in no wise decreased. "And he lowered himself very much in my opinion by that silly speech of his the other night. He will find that his father will not support him in any such ideas, I feel sure of that. A young man who has to make his own way in the world and who needs strong friends to help him, as Philip Nelson does, would appear much better if he didn't try to take the lead in new notions. In any case, he ought to know enough to keep his half-fledged opinions to himself. However, I don't know that Philip Nelson and his opinions are of interest to us. I don't know why we should waste our time in discussing him."

Margaret laughed and was about to reply, but a glance just then at David's face held her silent.

To the surprise of all, it was the generally quiet, easily led mother who took up the word. "That seems to me a very strange way to talk. Philip has been intimate with us ever since he was a child, and we have all liked him very much. I don't know why he shouldn't be allowed to express his opinions. He is old enough to form opinions certainly, and I'm sure he has shown very good sense in doing so in the past."

"Let him keep from expressing them in my house then," interrupted her husband loudly. "I want none of his opinions, if they are as foolish and harmful as those he advanced the other night. I simply am *not* going to have my name mixed up with this folly and sin, and anyone who wishes to be reckoned as a child of mine has to understand it."

His audience had increased again. Frances, work in hand, had seated herself on the doorstep and was keenly alive to every word that was being spoken.

But it was the look on David's face, not hers, that quickened the mother into speech again. "Father, you forget that David is not a little boy anymore.

He has been sick for so long, and we have been so used to thinking of and caring for him as helpless, that we all forget that he is a man with rights of his own."

Mr. Holman turned toward his wife in uncontrollable irritation.

"Hannah, what is the matter with you? We have lived together for more years than David's life, and I never knew you before to consider it necessary to oppose every word I said. At least, if I were you, I would try not to do it in the presence of the children. If David were a hundred years old, instead of thirty, and was still a member of my family, dependent upon me for support, I would think it incumbent upon him to respect my views and be guided by my wishes. Unless he is a great deal less of a man than I take him to be, he agrees with me."

Thus appealed to, David rose from the seat beside his mother, laying down the spool and scissors. As he did so he gave her a wonderfully sweet and reassuring smile. To his father he said gently, "I remember, sir, that you said you were very tired. Perhaps we have talked as long as we should. It's the hour for family worship. At another time I'd be glad if you would allow me to talk with you about this and other matters. But I shouldn't weary you further tonight. In the meantime, I will try not to fail in the respect and consideration due you."

As he was speaking, he crossed the room for the family Scriptures and laid them on his father's knee. Then he gathered the sewing from his mother's hand and bent and kissed her flushed cheek. The father, subduing his agitation as best he could, opened the Scriptures at random and read the words upon which his eyes first rested, those of the prophet Isaiah. "Who hath believed our report?

and to whom is the arm of the Lord revealed?... He is despised and rejected of men; a man of sorrows, and acquainted with grief: and we hid as it were our faces from him."

Very soon thereafter David and Frances were alone in the little yard opening from the side door. Frances had slipped away first, and David had followed, as he often did when he wanted a word with her alone. They were silent, however, for several minutes.

"Well," said David at last, as he laid a comforting hand on his sister's shoulder, "you see how it is. It is becoming very plain, is it not, that some of us will have to face opposition of no common order?"

"If only Margaret could have been more considerate!" said Frances. "Why did she need to mention Philip's name, when she saw what a state Father was in? It really seems, at times, as though Margaret — "

She abruptly checked herself, leaving the sentence unfinished.

David regarded her thoughtfully. "How is it that Margaret seems to have so little sympathy with you in this matter?" he asked. "Or rather, how is it that she has such a different impression? Do you suppose it can be the influence of Masters?"

"I'm afraid so. I think she has heard more from him than she cares to tell. She seems strangely prejudiced. In some respects she is almost more bitter than Father. What can it be but his influence? She has suspected Philip, I think, for some time. She asked me if it was Philip's influence that made me so silent about the step you took. But of course she heard from his own lips the other night where he stands."

"I was thoughtless myself tonight," David said regretfully. "I shouldn't have started the conversation in that direction by my news. But it all seemed so wonderful and so blessed to me that I confess I forgot how it would appear to my father. Were you there, Frances, when I told about Michael Payne's recovery? It was such a glorious thing to see him in his right mind and in splendid physical condition! It seemed as if it was something for which we could all rejoice together."

"It is," agreed Frances quietly. "I heard your words, David, though I had not yet come downstairs. Of course you couldn't help telling it. A stone would have spoken if it had known poor Michael's condition but a few days ago. Besides, we can't go on in this way. We might as well be outspoken; some definite step must be taken. Why not now as well as any time? If we only knew just what is right!"

Her brother felt almost startled by her words. She seemed to have taken long strides in a single night. Was she possibly ahead of him?

"Some definite step!" he repeated. "Just what do you mean, dear?"

"I hardly know. Nothing is clear to me as yet. Only...when a man is...such a man as he is proving himself to be; has not only physical help to give, but instruction as well; and has a definite following and is willing to have it, mustn't one sooner or later declare for or against him and take the consequences?"

David drew a long breath. "You have moved ahead rapidly, Frances. And as yet you have never even seen him!"

"No, but Philip has. And I haven't moved rapidly; on the contrary I have been slow. So slow and cautious that at times I've been ashamed of myself. I have heard a great deal about him, David, and yet our timid little mother seems to have more courage to speak for him than I have! But to me it is fraught with such consequences. Philip thinks — "

She made one of her abrupt pauses, like one who was indeed going too fast.

David's hand that held her own tightened its clasp as he asked, "Is there an engagement, dear?"

"No, only an understanding. I couldn't engage myself without my father's consent."

"And that under present circumstances he would not give," David said with a heavy sigh. "It is indeed growing complicated!"

"David, what does the man ask or expect of those who call themselves his pupils?"

"I don't know. Some of them, as you know, follow him about wherever he goes. But he can't expect that of all his friends; it would be impossible. Moreover, there is a large class following him now who cannot be called his friends. If enough motive were offered, I think they would promptly become his enemies. But you're right about the definite step that must be taken soon, or at least there must be definite knowledge on the part of those who would own him. Perhaps we're imagining it to be more difficult than it will be. We don't positively know that he desires anything but to help people all he can. Perhaps his is a beautiful, unselfish, perfect life, hidden in God and revealed to us suddenly for us to see what real companionship with God might do for us. God may have given him certain miraculous powers so that his work may help us to have full confidence in His word. Such men used to be, Frances — why not again?"

"Like one of the old prophets?" said Frances.

"Yes, I've thought of that. Of course, I don't know anything about it, but there are times when I can't help thinking, or rather feeling, that he is much more than that."

"How could he be more than that, my dear sister?"

But Frances had no more words to say. She persisted that she knew nothing, understood nothing, that mere "feeling" is not to be trusted in any case; and he was much better able to judge these things than she was. For the present, she supposed there was nothing for them to do but wait and be as quiet as their sense of honor would allow.

"Meanwhile, David," she added eagerly, as one who was resolved upon an entire change of subject, "tell me what you're going to do? About yourself, I mean? You're not satisfied to work in the fields, are you? To give your life to such work, with your education and talent?"

"No," he said. That, he agreed, would hardly be right, even though he might desire it. There were times when he shrank from the thought of the world and felt as though the open fields, working among God's gifts to man, would be of all labor the most desirable. But his education had been too expensive to be used in that way, and besides, there were other times when he longed to be out among men, exerting an influence upon the crowds.

He was going into town soon, as soon indeed as he had positively settled certain matters connected with the talk they had just been having. Probably he should take up his studies where he had left them and carry out his first intentions of becoming a lawyer. He was late, it was true, and had lost a great deal of time. But he did not feel it was all wasted. He had done better work some of the time while lying on his back than he had ever succeeded in doing when in health.

Then he broke off suddenly from these slow, detached sentences which his sister could feel were taking only half his thought and began to speak rapidly: "I'll tell you the whole truth, Frances. Before I decide anything, I mean to see and have a long talk with this stranger who has come so suddenly and powerfully into my life. I am strangely drawn toward him. It's not remarkable either, when I realize what he has done for me. Of course, it's the most natural feeling in the world — even my father realizes it. But I mean much more than those words convey. I also have a feeling of awe regarding him, such as no one has ever inspired in me. Despite what I've just been saying to you, I believe in my soul that he has come among us for more than a mere object lesson of purity and unselfishness. My father would call it a superstition. But the belief that this man has something further to do with my life, that it is indeed linked in some strange way to his life, grows upon me."

"Superstition? How could it be superstition," asked Frances, "when these experiences and beliefs are shared by those we know and trust? Philip believes it, and the belief grows stronger every day. I can see that the influence, whatever it is, increases powerfully upon him. That's what has made me think that possibly — "

She broke off nervously, catching her breath as one who felt almost afraid.

"I wish you would tell me plainly just what you think, dear, and not lead me to grope blindly along the road where your swifter intuitions have carried you."

"Oh, David, I *dare* not. At times my half-frightened thoughts seem to me to be rank blasphemy! I couldn't put them into words. I have no reasons for them which would justify my speaking. Remember, I have never seen the man. How much I wish that I could!"

"Ah! I can't tell you how much I wish that, too! If it weren't for this bitter prejudice, we could invite him to our home and talk with him freely until we understood. Sometimes the thought overwhelms me, that the man who gave me back to life is a stranger to my father and mother and remains so by their — at least by Father's — choice."

"Poor Father!" bemoaned Frances. He can't help his prejudices; they are a part of his life. If Mr. Masters hadn't poured out his intolerable platitudes for Father to lean on, it might have been different. I am afraid of that man and of his influence in our family — and over Margaret most of all. Oh, David! Can't we save her from him in some way? I'm sure he is bad."

"Poor little burden-bearer!" said David tenderly, passing his strong arm about her. "She needs someone to carry her burdens for her. It all comes back to the one theme, dear: I wish you knew *him*. You *must* know him."

CHAPTER IX

HE THAT
SOWETH INIQUITY
SHALL REAP
VANITY

they paced back and forth for several minutes in silence, with David's protective arm still about his sister. At last he broke the silence. There was a changed quality to his voice. It suggested one who had admitted a new train of thought that was full of meaning for him but that he was holding himself well in check.

"Frances, do you know anything of Miriam Brownlee?"

"I haven't seen her for many months, but I often hear of her. She's here with her aunt, you know."

He gave an involuntary start, and she could feel his arm tremble. All he said was, "I didn't know it."

"Philip saw her last week. He had occasion to go there on business. He says she is as beautiful as ever, and he imagines quite as happy. David, I didn't know whether to speak of her to you or not."

The brother smiled gravely. "You thought you might touch a sore nerve?" he asked.

Frances, who did not know how to reply to that, was silent for a moment. But David seemed to have no more to say, so she ventured a question: "Do you mean to call there?"

"I think so. One hardly knows how to plan after a blank of so many years." He waited some time before adding his next sentence. "It may surprise you to know that the last time I called at Mr. Brownlee's, he ordered me from the house."

"David!"

"It was right," he said, answering the indignation her tones expressed. "I could bear him no ill will for that; I should have been ordered out. I went there in such a condition that a gentleman who had regard for the ladies of his household could do no less. I had been drinking, Frances. I wasn't exactly intoxicated; at least I hadn't thought so, as you may be sure. But I was more thoroughly under the influence of liquor than I had ever been before, and I evidently didn't know how I looked or what I was saying. I remember his words, however; they cut into my soul. He told me to go home and remain there until I knew how to conduct myself as a gentleman should, that at present I was no better than a brute. He didn't know how literally I would obey him, nor how many years it would take."

His sister gave a startled cry. "Oh, David! Was it on the night that you were hurt?"

"Yes. The condition I was in was the main cause
of the accident, I presume, though I think the horse
would have been frightened under the circumstances anyway. I might have been able to control
him if I had been myself. Besides being insane with
liquor, I was insane with passion. I understood my
condition so little as to believe that I had been insulted. But I long ago exonerated Mr. Brownlee
from all blame."

"But, David, he was one of the first who called
after you were brought home. He called again and
again while you were at the worst and was most
kind and thoughtful to us all."

"I know — I remember him perfectly. I used to
think that he possibly felt some responsibility for
the accident. He must have seen I was in no condition to drive down that dangerous road, certainly
not to drive that horse. However, as I say, I don't
blame him. I don't know what else he could have
done. I've always been glad that I brought myself
to the point of seeing him once when he called and
telling him that I thought he did quite right."

"I don't think he did right at all," stated Frances
positively, adding immediately: "But, David, you
remember that he's gone, don't you?"

"Oh, yes, I recall vividly the circumstances connected with his death. It seemed so strange to me
that he should be taken in the prime of life, when
his business and family and the world at large
would miss him so sorely, and I, a useless hulk, a
sorrow to my friends and a misery to myself,
should be left! We don't understand the ways of
our Father, do we? And yet we are always trying to
plan for Him!

"Mr. Brownlee's absence complicates my embar-
rassments. If he were there, so I might go and ask if

he would receive me at his house again, my way would be plain. As it is, I think I will venture. One can't know how the family will feel. They must have known all about the matter at the time. Still, if Miriam is there, I must certainly make the attempt. To do less might even be counted as dishonorable. I don't know how much difference time makes. Can you help me, dear? Do you know anything about Miriam's life? At least she isn't married?"

"Oh, no! There have been reports from time to time. But each report had her name coupled with a different person, so that I've never known what to think, except what others say of her: that she is fickle in her tastes. I used to think that — is she in any way bound to you, David?"

"Not at all. If she had been, she would have been freed long ago, remember."

Frances wanted to ask more questions, but her brother's grave, sad manner held her back. How much did he care for Miriam Brownlee? Her heart sank within her as she asked herself the question. She had hoped and at times had believed that he had forgotten Miriam, or at least that she had lost power to hurt him. On this evening something in his manner, rather than his words, told her differently. Could there be any real, lasting sympathy between these two? She hadn't understood the attraction, even in her brother's happy youth; much less did she understand it now. She tried to check her unflattering thoughts of the girl and told herself that she was doubtless prejudiced by what others said, that she had little acquaintance with her and shouldn't judge. Perhaps, if she came to know her better, she would feel differently. But on the whole she decided that she would ask no more questions. She did not want David to commit himself in words to any position that had to do with Miriam Brownlee.

What he felt, he kept in great measure to himself. He had only hinted at the embarrassment of his position. He felt it very keenly when, on the evening following this conversation, he found himself sitting in the familiar parlor of the Brownlee home, waiting to see what reception would be given to his card. Everything about him was as lovely and as natural as ever. It seemed incredible that a gulf of years had intervened since he had last sat there!

The Brownlees were an old, aristocratic family. Their ancestry, at least on Mrs. Brownlee's side, dated back so far that only she cared to study it out. The husband, if not able to trace his pedigree so far, had been able to furnish the means with which to give his wife's pride a beautiful setting. Everywhere in and around the fine old place was that lavish expenditure which is, or ought to be, evidence of abundant means.

There were no daughters to grace this elegant home. The father, dying three years before the date at which our story opens, had left his young son, not yet of age, prospective heir to a princely fortune. He had not, however, forgotten his favorite niece, Miriam, who was the daughter of his widowed sister. She belonged to a home where daughters were numerous, and therefore she was often spared to the uncle and aunt who adored her.

Here David Holman had met her, when he was himself but a boy. A very ardent friendship had sprung up between the two. As the years went by, no guest was welcomed more frequently and cordially to the elegant home than the young man David Holman. He was not wealthy, it is true. But he belonged to one of the oldest of the fine old families and was reported to have an unusually brilliant mind. "The sort of man," Mr. Brownlee was fond of saying, "who is sure to make his mark in the world, as soon as he gets beyond the indiscretions of youth."

Moreover, he was fine-looking, had polished manners and was always well dressed. What mattered it that there were whispers of his being a trifle fast? That belonged to those aforesaid "indiscretions of youth." He was certainly charming in conversation. What more should a family desire who were not themselves deeply interested in religion and who liked nothing better than being entertained?

That his beautiful niece Miriam was the special attraction to his home, Mr. Brownlee seemed to know, and to offer no objection. At least, when his wife hinted at possible complications, he replied that young women in these days knew how to take care of themselves in such matters, and he would trust Miriam where he wouldn't himself. She certainly might form worse friendships for life than one with the Holman family. No syllable could be breathed against them or their ancestors. And David was smart enough to make his way in the world and sharp enough not to bring discredit on the honored family name.

Yes, he knew he was inclined to be rather too lively. Young men just out of college were likely to make that mistake, but David was too levelheaded and had had too good a backing for generations to go far astray. He would trust him. And he did trust him, until David walked nearer the edge of ruin than any of them realized.

The past, with all its opportunities and possibilities and almost infinite blunders, came back clearly to the young man who sat once more surrounded by the pictures and other furnishings he had often studied while waiting. Looked at from one point of view, what an eternity of years separated him from those periods of waiting! His face burned again, as it had often before, over the vivid memory of that evening when, for the first time in his life, he had appeared in society sufficiently under the influence of liquor to be, not brilliant, but silly.

He recalled some of his words as distinctly as though it were an event of yesterday. They were not so glaringly improper as they might have been, but enough to cause Mrs. Brownlee's laugh to be very constrained. Her look plainly said that she was not quite sure whether to laugh or frown. He blessed the memory of Mr. Brownlee because he had realized his condition and ordered him from the house before Miriam appeared. But of course it had all been explained to her. Now, after the lapse even of so many years, could she help thinking at once of that last time?

He had caught a single glimpse of her on that evening long ago, as she flitted through the hall just as he mounted the piazza steps. He had heard her silvery laugh in response to some sally of her boy cousin's; then she had vanished up the stairs, and the unexpected years had stretched between them!

And she was the woman whom he had hoped to make his wife. Long before this date, on which he sat waiting and wondering whether she would even give him audience, he had planned to have been settled in a beautiful house of his own. Of course, his career in life was to be eminently successful; he had always planned that. He meant to

surround her with fully as many comforts and
luxuries as she found in her uncle's home. Sometimes his ambition and imagination carried him far
beyond such modest elegance and made a very
palace for his queen.

On that ill-fated night, before he took that second glass of liquor, he had planned to see Miriam
alone and learn definitely from her own lips that
she understood him and was ready to wait for him.

He remembered that he had felt very little fear
as to what her answer would be. She had seemed
to be entirely frank in her appreciation of him, despite the ugly stories concerning his habits which
were more or less afloat. He thought of the stories
then; he remembered and blushed over them and
assured himself that if Miriam's answer to his appeal was what he believed it would be, it would
mark an entirely new era in his life. He would
break forever with the unsafe associates he had followed into danger and give himself seriously to
the work of building up an entirely different reputation. He owed that to Miriam, he told himself.

So sure had he been of her answer to the question he meant to ask that he had said, as he lifted
that fatal glass of liquor to his lips, "Boys, I'm going to reform; this is to bid you good-bye. It is my
last glass."

The boys had shouted over what they looked
upon as a good joke, but the words had been ominously true. No drop of liquor since that hour had
passed David Holman's lips.

It seems natural to speak of that as "the fatal
glass." Under its influence the young man went
out to an experience of long, slow torture that had
seemed to him a hundred times worse than death.
The only door of escape at the end he had sup-

posed to be the door of death. Yet if he had seen the map of his life spread out before him, he might have gone on his knees in gratitude to God for being left to drink that last glass. Since he *would not* be led in any other way, a merciful God led him through the fire.

But his resolution to reform? Sitting there, waiting, after the furnace was behind him, David Holman smiled gravely over the memory of his weak resolve and realized how little it had meant on the lips of one who could toy with it as he had done.

The weary years had moved slowly on. Miriam Brownlee, with those words left unsaid that were to have held her to him, was free to do as she would — and was Miss Brownlee still. And at last, *at last*, he was sitting in that well-remembered spot waiting for her!

Not with the old words trembling on his lips — he had no sense of assurance now. He felt that he would not be surprised nor have cause to complain even if she refused to come in response to his card. He had forfeited long ago the right to consideration from her.

Yet her uncle had forgiven him. More than once he had brought baskets of lovely flowers, which he said "the ladies" sent. David, as he fingered the delicate blooms, had felt in his soul that Miriam had sent them. It was like her, and the flowers were like her, delicate and pure and faithful. In his direct pain those flowers had comforted him.

But Mr. Brownlee was gone, and any lingering hope that his friends might have felt that David would be among them again had died long ago. He had gone as completely out of the world as though the grave had closed over him. Even the name of Miriam Brownlee had not been mentioned to him for years. Frances had dropped it entirely, at first because she realized that the mention excited her patient. Afterward, when Miriam had left the neighborhood and returned to her own home, it was easy for the girl to forget her; she hoped that her brother had done so.

David, as he went back over all these experiences, knew that he had not forgotten. Is it any wonder that, under such unusual circumstances, he felt his heart giving great throbs of anticipation, or of apprehension — he hardly knew which? Suddenly there was a rustle of drapery near at hand, a flutter of ribbons, a vision as of something wonderfully fair and familiar besides, and Miriam Brownlee stood before him.

CHAPTER X

Hear Ye Indeed, But Understand Not

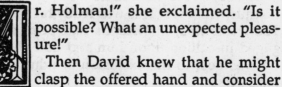r. Holman!" she exclaimed. "Is it possible? What an unexpected pleasure!"

Then David knew that he might clasp the offered hand and consider himself a welcome guest. Miriam's voice had qualities in it that he had studied in the past. It was capable of an almost infinite variety of meanings. He had heard it when he had told himself that if she should use such tones with him, he would know better than to call upon her ever again. She never had; she did not on this evening. He tried to study her critically while he talked. Philip had been right; she was as beautiful as ever. No, she was more beautiful. When he saw her last, it had been the changeful beauty of young girlhood. Now she stood before him a symmetrical development of beauty that no added touch could improve. She had more than fulfilled the promise of her youth.

"Certainly we have heard of you!" she said, sinking like a snowy cloud into the seat he moved forward for her. It seemed to him as if the pretty chair came up of itself and took her in its arms caressingly, rather than that she took possession of it. What an embodiment of grace she was!

"Certainly we have heard of you!" she repeated. "Do you think we live out of the world that we shouldn't know the wonders that absorb it? We have wondered, Auntie and I, that you should be so very long in remembering your old friends. We began to think you meant to ignore us altogether. But I suppose you have so many friends that we ought to have been content to await our turn."

Indeed, David assured her quickly he had made no calls whatever. This was really his first attempt. The truth was, his friends had been chiefly engaged in calling upon him and had absorbed his time, almost to the exclusion of other duties and pleasures.

"Is that the way?" she said lightly. "We might have ventured, perhaps, if we had understood it, but it isn't likely. Auntie makes very few calls indeed in these days. There have been sad changes here, Mr. Holman."

"Yes," David said and stopped. He could say no more. He found himself strangely embarrassed. She was the only person he had thought of being with in this world to which he had suddenly returned. It seemed impossible to talk with this lovely vision of the past as he had with others. All words sounded tame and entirely inadequate to the situation.

The lady, however, showed no trace of embarrassment. Her talk flowed on musically. Her guest found himself wondering if anything ever disturbed the satisfied world the center of which she seemed to be. How bright she was! How unchanged! Was she? Or had there been a very great change? He could not be sure.

Mrs. Brownlee came presently to offer him cordial welcome to her home. Nothing could be more cordial than her reception. Apparently there was no obstacle in the way of his dropping at once into his old place in their circle. Yet that indefinable feeling of possible change, at least in Miriam, haunted him. It was easier to talk after Mrs. Brownlee joined them. She referred promptly to the past, saying just enough to let her guest know what would be proper for him to say, then glided naturally into other topics.

David rallied his energy and talked in a way that went far toward establishing himself as he once had appeared in more favorable days; yet all the while he was conscious of carrying on a separate train of thought. He was studying Miriam, trying to place her — trying to place himself in relation to her. Had she understood him in the past as fully as he had believed? Had she felt toward him as he had imagined she did? But suppose she had? He had been the same as dead for years. Had the lady who was to have been so potent a factor in his life so far forgotten him that he must begin again almost as a new acquaintance? If so, was he ready to begin? In other words, was he unchanged? Not that, either. He felt almost as though resurrection itself could make no greater change in him than had already taken place. But did the change necessarily affect his relations toward Miriam?

Very important questions these, especially for him to consider while he was at the same time helping to carry on an animated conversation. Of course, he was not fully aware of the trend of his thoughts; put into words, they would have startled him. Meanwhile the conversation turned into channels that helped him mark some of the changes.

Miriam Brownlee and he had been living in different worlds, and this became apparent. He spoke of certain books. Many had been read to him; Frances had devoted hours each day to that purpose, making her selections carefully.

Miss Brownlee knew some of the books by their titles; two or three of them she had read. But the ones that he and Frances had lingered over and enjoyed the most, Miriam unhesitatingly pronounced stupid. They had bored her immensely, she said. She would never have attempted their reading, except that so many people were talking about them. As it was, she had skipped the moralizing as much as possible and also the descriptive parts; she hated description in books.

On being further pressed by the man who did not realize, and did not want to realize, that he was weighing her in the balance, she asked if a certain book that had been his special enjoyment was not almost of the "goody-goody sort." She considered such books the most complete bores that one could find. Suddenly she deserted the world of literature altogether and launched forth into a description of the last "season."

"We had a succession of charming evenings," she said. "Our particular set, I mean. For six or eight weeks I believe we were together nearly every evening. The season was unusually lively. Of

course, we danced a great deal. I remember how
fond you used to be of dancing. Dear me! How
very hard it must have been to be deprived of that
entertainment for so many years."

"Miriam!" her aunt exclaimed with a deprecat-
ing laugh. "What a child you are! I don't believe
you will ever grow up. Think of Mr. Holman suffering as intensely as we have heard that he did
and giving any of his thought to deprivations in
that direction!"

"Why not?" Miriam asked, opening wide her
beautiful eyes in a childishly innocent way that
used to charm her caller. "That was part of the suffering, I presume. I am sure it would be with me.
Confess, Mr. Holman — didn't you often long to be
among us indulging in your favorite amusement?"

David listened almost as one in a dream. Dancing! Yes, he certainly used to dance — in fact, as
this vision before him said, used to be very fond of
that amusement. How utterly it had gone out, not
only of his life, but his thoughts! His sisters were
not dancers, and the one with whom he had had
most to do never seemed even to remember there
was such an occupation. Evidently there were two
very distinct worlds here on earth. Would it be impossible to intermingle them comfortably? If so,
did he dwell in one and Miriam Brownlee in the
other? The question flashed itself before his troubled thoughts, but he refused to notice it.

At that moment Mrs. Brownlee was summoned
from the room, and Miriam turned toward him,
another Miriam, rather, the old one. There was a
softened light in her beautiful eyes and a gentle
quality in her voice as she said, "It seems very
strange, and yet very natural, to see you sitting
here in the old place. Have you the least idea, I

wonder, how glad we are to welcome you back?"

Instantly his heart told him she was unchanged. This lovely, self-poised woman was the Miriam of his dreams. That cheerful, almost heartless tone and volatile manner had doubtless been assumed to cover deeper feeling. If they could have opportunity to talk alone together for a few minutes, it was plain that she would show him another self. But Mrs. Brownlee returned after a moment, and the talk flowed on as before. David, who believed that now he understood, did not feel so jarred by its volatile character as he had been. But suddenly a subject was introduced in such a manner that it seemed to him like laying bare a nerve and playing with it. It was Miriam, too, who began it.

"Oh! Have you been back in the world long enough to have heard of our latest sensation? It's unique, I assure you."

With a smile he expressed his ignorance, all unprepared for what was to follow.

"Why, we have a seer, a prophet — a second-sight, second-touch man. What shall I name our sensation, Auntie? Have you really never heard of him, Mr. Holman? They call him a physician. He has honored my own town with a visit of several weeks' duration. He moves through the streets followed by the most motley crowd that ever helped to form a procession. The lower classes, you know, decidedly. The blind and hungry and lame and lazy — they are all there. Beggars without number, and a class even lower on the social scale than beggars. The very worst classes have taken to following him about.

"Somehow the notion has gone abroad that he can cure all ordinary, or for that matter extraordinary, ailments, as well as feed the hungry, even

without food! He seems able to rise above such
trivialities. The most extraordinary stories are
afloat concerning him. One realizes as one listens
to them the utter credulity of the ignorant world.
Why, there are those who say the man has some
sort of supernatural power. And the number of
people who fancy themselves cured by him of
some malady or other is increasing daily."

"Miriam!" Mrs. Brownlee succeeded at last in
arresting the voluble tongue. She had tried in vain
to catch her niece's eye. At last her voice, almost
sharp, swept into the current of words.

"Miriam! Is it possible that you do not remember? If half of what we have heard is true, Mr. Holman must have much more knowledge of this
remarkable man than we have."

For a moment Miriam was evidently discomfit-
ted. She glanced from David's pale face to her
aunt's annoyed one and seemed not to know what
to say next.

Mrs. Brownlee attempted to help her. "Had you
forgotten, dear child, that our friend's wonderful
cure is attributed by outsiders to the aid of the very
person about whom you are talking?"

"Why, Auntie, I have heard that absurd story, of
course. But I didn't attach any importance to it, any
more than I supposed other sensible people did.
It's only imaginary ailments that that man cures.
Mr. Holman, you have no idea that he had anything to do with it, have you?"

For a single moment David hesitated — not as to
what he should say, but as to how he should say it.
Much self-control was necessary in order to reply
quietly to such a question. When he spoke, the
very quietness of his voice may have misled them,
though the words were positive enough. "On the

contrary, Miss Brownlee, I have every reason to believe that it is entirely because of that remarkable man's power and blessed intervention that I am not lying helpless tonight on the bed where I have spent so many years."

"Is it possible?" exclaimed both ladies at once.

Miriam hastened to add, "We hadn't given a moment's credence to the story. From the very first, I thought there must be a scientific explanation of the cure, and then — who was telling us, Auntie? Oh, I remember. It was Mr. Masters. Have you met him, Mr. Holman? The nephew of Governor Masters. He's a highly educated young man, a lawyer.

"He told us he thought your experience would be a remarkably interesting one for medical students. He said it was believed that nature had effected a cure, all unknown to you. Being carried for so long a distance in the open air, together with the discovery that you could really endure the motion, after having for so long believed all motion to be impossible for you, proved to be such a tonic that your unused willpower asserted itself and commanded your limbs into action. I haven't told it as he did. He was very scientific, I assure you, but that's the idea. We were very much interested, weren't we, Auntie? We thought it the most remarkable experience we had ever heard of."

"That's not surprising," said David quietly. "Such an explanation is undoubtedly remarkable, but it is also incorrect in every detail."

Mrs. Brownlee's voice interposed. "Miriam, dear, you didn't quite do Mr. Masters justice. Do you remember how careful he was to impress us with the fact that Mr. Holman's contact with that remarkable man certainly had its effect? A sort of mesmeric effect, you know, only used in a good cause, as mesmeric effects so often are not. He said the will of the stronger man was projected into that of the pain-weakened one and compelled it to assert itself. Those were his very words, Mr. Holman. I thought it extremely interesting."

"I'd forgotten that part," said Miriam carelessly. "I haven't so much taste for abstruse scientific points as you have, Auntie. But I remember now that I thought if Mr. Holman was in the least like the gentleman of that name with whom I used to be well acquainted, he had willpower enough to move the world, whenever he chose to exert it. But, Mr. Holman, really, you have no idea of the ridiculous lengths which the people have gone in their superstitions about this entire stranger. By 'the people' I mean, of course, the crowd, the rabble, the slums. He seems to have almost no friends among the better classes."

Once more Mrs. Brownlee interposed. "Oh, my dear! Some of his followers are at least respectable. And you know we've heard he visits at the Rothwells'."

"Yes, Auntie, we have heard it, as we have heard a great many other odd things. I have no faith whatever in that report. The Rothwells are very exclusive."

"Who are the Rothwells?" demanded David, catching at the new name as a relief. He must have a respite with unimportant ground on which to rest for a moment, until he could control his indignation and determine what it was wise to say next.

Miriam's reply was ready. "Haven't you heard of the Rothwells? They're newcomers, new at least since you left the world. I have the honor to claim them as fellow-townspeople. They have bought the old Symonds place, a mile or so out of town.

You remember it? A very aristocratic old place, and they are very aristocratic people. Indeed, I believe the place was connected with their family in some way. The married sister is a Mrs. Symonds.

"You'll have to know them, Mr. Holman. I assure you it is quite the thing to do. The family is composed of a brother and two sisters; the aforesaid Mrs. Symonds, a widow, being one. The other is Miss Mary Rothwell, and she and her brother are both very interesting. He's handsome and learned and — well, everything that the best people fancy. I've heard he's a trifle too grave, but I don't think so. Gravity is refreshing in a young man. It suggests such a contrast to the ordinary.

"His young sister, Mary, is a perfect rosebud — at least, that's what the young men call her, with rare promise for the opening flower. That's a poetical bit for which I'm indebted to Mr. Masters. I laughed at him, however. I told him I thought she deserved to be considered a flower already. She is by no means so young as people think. At least, I don't believe she is. I wouldn't place her a day below twenty-three, and I wouldn't be surprised if she were twenty-five. She's probably older than she looks; girls of her type nearly always are.

"You'll be charmed with her, Mr. Holman — everybody is, every gentleman — though I remember you never liked the rosebud style of woman. I think personally there is too little variety about either her face or character to be interesting for any great length of time."

The subject seemed to have uncommon interest for Miriam. David hardly heard her words; one sentence had caught and held his thoughts. At this new home the stranger was said sometimes to visit.

CHAPTER XI

THERE IS
NO BEAUTY
THAT WE SHOULD
DESIRE HIM

When an opportunity presented itself for words, he asked a question. "Did I understand you to say that this stranger visits at the Rothwells'?"

"That's the common report. But as I've been saying to you, I don't credit it. The Rothwells are the most aristocratic family we have, and he — well, you know what he is. But I can't think that you realize for a moment the class of people with whom he constantly mingles. He has gathered a company of very intimate friends who are always with him, day and night, for all I know. They tramp over the country holding street meetings and doing all sorts of odd things. What must a man be who chooses his most intimate friends

111

from such sources? They are all, without exception, from the very commonest classes."

The more temperate aunt found it necessary to keep holding her niece in check. "My dear," she said, "didn't we hear that Philip Nelson was one of the group who travel with him?"

"I believe so, Auntie, but that was probably mere gossip. You and I don't believe all we hear, remember. Philip was always an erratic sort of person, but he would hardly stoop so low as that. You should know, Mr. Holman. Isn't he quite intimate with your family? Do you really think he has been beguiled into this new superstition?"

"He considers the man we've been talking about to be a most uncommon friend." David said this with exceeding dignity, but he chose his words with great care. He was growing more and more sure that this man's friends had no pleasant path to tread. For Philip's sake he must speak with caution.

Miriam gave a gentle little sigh as she replied, "Well, it's certainly very sad to think how easily people are duped. I hope Philip Nelson will discover his foolishness in time to prevent unpleasant results. I always liked the young man. Of course, one may be interested and curious and like to study new ideas, as I presume you are doing. But to follow the man about and allow one's name to be constantly coupled with his is quite another matter. Pardon the interference, Mr. Holman, but I should think you would feel like giving Philip a friendly warning — although, of course, you haven't had time to understand the state of things. It's really growing dreadful! Why, at home the streets are sometimes impassable because of the crowds around the house where that man stops.

And such a crowd!"

"Have you ever seen the man?" interrupted David.

"I? Oh, no, indeed! Mother would be shocked beyond rallying if I were to venture into the streets at all when the crowd is swarming. I assure you, I have no desire to see him. I don't understand why the authorities don't interfere to prevent his doing further mischief. They shake their heads, and their faces convey thoughts they cannot speak. But so far as I can tell, they do nothing."

Her guest was holding himself well in check, but it was not in human nature not to ask one question more. "But, Miss Brownlee, enlighten me. What has the stranger done to arouse the displeasure or the fears of respectable people? I have heard only of his relieving suffering wherever he found it. There is surely nothing in such acts to challenge the interference of the authorities."

Miss Brownlee shrugged her shapely shoulders. "Oh, don't ask me! You must talk with someone who is better posted about public affairs. I only know that some deep political intrigue is more than suspected, aiming at an insurrection or some horror of that sort. Why, I think it's very harmful to gather together the worst classes of humanity and play upon their credulity to secure an influence over them; one could then move them in whatever direction he chose, when his scheme was ripe. Even a woman can foresee danger under such conditions, Mr. Holman. Doesn't it impress you so?"

"Which part of your statement?" said David, allowing the semblance of a smile to appear for an instant on his grave face. "How to get a controlling influence over the lower classes of society is a problem which the best people in our cities have long been studying. If the influence is used for good, I can conceive of nothing more important."

"Well, I assure you that the best people fear this man and know that the result will be anything but good. You should talk with Mr. Masters. He understands the situation perfectly and is really very anxious about it. Auntie, don't you remember what an excitement he worked himself into the other evening, talking to those friends of John's who were here? That reminds me of one of the stories afloat. The whole matter has its ludicrous side, I think — though people like Mr. Masters, who have to be patriots all the time, refuse to see it. John came home one evening, much excited over a story of a wedding reception held in some town near here; I forget the name — no matter. The important part is that the caterers had made a mistake as to the quantity of wine, and it gave out before half the guests were served. This remarkable performer turned a large amount of spring water into wine! It would be economical to have him for a friend, would it not?"

David rose abruptly. There was a look in his eyes that might have suggested to Miss Brownlee the David Holman she used to know when something had roused him to indignation. He made his adieus rapidly, notwithstanding the evident surprise and equally evident disappointment of the ladies over the early departure.

Mrs. Brownlee followed him to the hall and made an effort to soothe the nerves that she felt, rather than saw, had been disturbed. "Miriam chatters on like the child that she is," she said, "despite the dignity of the added years since you last saw her. She has heard so much about this new superstition or interest — I hardly know by what name to speak of it — and has been so annoyed by several little experiences connected with it that it has made her somewhat harsh in her judgment. Still, I confess that there are features about it calculated to make thoughtful people anxious.

"For instance, my John has become so excited over the stories he hears that it has required all his mother's influence — to say nothing of almost commands — to keep him from joining the promiscuous crowds who follow that strange man about. Sometimes I'm very troubled over what the outcome may be. It is my anxiety, I guess, that has made Miriam so emphatic. I must admit that I hoped you could advise us as to what course we should take with John. After you've studied the subject thoroughly, Mr. Holman, as I feel sure for the interests of the country you will do, perhaps you'll talk with John. He's only a boy yet, you know."

It was well for David Holman that a long ride lay before him. He needed the influence of the night and the solitude to help him back to the point where he could think dispassionately. As he guided his horse carefully down the steep hillside, he recalled vividly that other ride which had ended so disastrously. He could scarcely have been more disturbed on that night long ago than he was at this time, but the two experiences were as far removed as the poles. There was no danger now of driving off the steep hillside into the ravine below; his brain was perfectly clear, yet his whole soul seemed to be in a tumult. He had never in his life been so humiliated, so wounded in the deepest feelings of his heart. Not the least of his bewilderment was that he did not understand the reason for this intense feeling.

Why should light, careless words concerning a man he had seen but once have power to sting and burn, to make him feel as though a hand he loved had reached forward and given him a mortal wound?

However, before he had traveled over the miles that separated him from his father's house, he reached a calmer mood — a mood in which he could assure himself that he had been unreasonable. It was not strange that Miss Brownlee should feel and speak as she did about an utter stranger, all knowledge of whom she had gained from sources likely only to prejudice her.

Several facts must be taken into consideration. It was not heartlessness but a dangerous talent she had for seeing the ludicrous side which had evoked those mocking words that stung him the most. Moreover, she was, as Mrs. Brownlee had hinted, troubled about her young cousin. From her point of view it would of course be disastrous to have the boy, on whom such fond hopes were centered and upon whom such heavy responsibilities of wealth would devolve, join a traveling doctor and roam over the country with him. Not that there was really danger of John's doing any such thing. But undoubtedly the mother was anxious and had communicated her anxiety to her niece. Also, he must remember that Miriam could not know what this stranger was to him —

At this point he was conscious of making what may be called a distinct pause in his thoughts. He realized that there was a question confronting him that must be answered before he could go further in any direction. What was this stranger to him? That he should be grateful to him beyond expression was a matter of course. It was even natural

under the circumstances for him to resent slighting
words spoken of him and that he should be indignant over hints of him as a dangerous person.

But all this could not account for the singular,
and he had to realize steadily increasing, influence
which the stranger exerted over him. He had tried
to resist this influence, to attribute it to an over-
wrought nervous temperament, to rise above it as
a sort of sentimentality; albeit he was aware that
whatever faults he might have, an inclination toward sentimentality had never been one of them.
Instead of putting aside the feeling, as the days
passed and he grew more accustomed to being out
in the world, he saw that it was unquestionably
gathering force from day to day — until to be with
that stranger, to hear his words and to follow his
instructions seemed to be the most important duty
in life.

Two things were definitely settled by the time he
reined in his horse at the home gateway: He would
suspend further judgment and, if possible, further
thought with regard to Miriam Brownlee until he
understood both himself and her better than he felt
that he now did. And he would, with as little delay
as possible, see and hear for himself this strange
teacher, selecting a time when he might consider
himself an unprejudiced, dispassionate observer.

To one other point he also gave a few minutes'
thought. Several times during his call, Miriam had
referred to Mr. Masters in a manner to lead one to
infer that he might be an intimate acquaintance.
Was he possibly more than that? And if so, was
there a hint in this of possible coming sorrow for
his sister Margaret? Though he felt his pulses
quicken over these questions, he made an earnest
effort to keep himself entirely in the background

and think only of Margaret.

After careful consideration, he felt assured that he believed Masters to be merely an acquaintance, who had distinguished himself by giving learned dissertations calculated to explain scientifically certain remarkable recoveries from what was thought to be mortal illness. He recalled the fact that Miriam had not at first remembered who her informant was. He then smiled gravely, perhaps a trifle sadly, to discover what infinite satisfaction this little item gave him. The final conclusion was that it was not possible for Masters ever to be more to Miriam Brownlee than a passing acquaintance, because she was so infinitely superior to him. Whether this conclusion was particularly flattering to his sister Margaret, he did not stop to consider but dismissed the whole subject from his thoughts.

For the next two or three days, David Holman, outwardly busy in the graperies with his father during an unusually crowded season, was in reality planning carefully the first steps of his future course. Foremost among his resolves remained that one — to see the physician who had cured him.

He had learned definitely that the man was staying in the neighboring city, which was Miriam Brownlee's home. A short journey would take him to the place, but there were difficulties in the way. He desired above all things to spare his father and mother, and especially Frances, unnecessary pain. How to arrange even so short an absence as would be necessary, without stating definitely his object, perplexed him.

He recognized that his long illness and the consequent care it had demanded had taught his family to think and feel about him much as they would

about a child left in their care. They could not be
expected to learn suddenly that he was a man and
must be allowed to plan his life without other
questionings than that which family ties usually
warrant. He also recognized the truth of his father's words, though they had cut him deeply
when they were spoken: He was still dependent
upon the home for his daily bread; and, at least so
long as this was the case, he ought to be governed
as far as possible by his father's judgment.

But for how long will this be possible? he asked
himself with a heavy sigh. To carry out his present
resolves seemed to be the first necessity of life. To
explain their nature boldly to his family would
bring discussion and heartache, possibly actual
rupture. He had rarely seen his father so roused
and so bitter.

He stood in the doorway of the little sitting
room at the close of a busy day. He was sorrowfully considering the problem that he saw no way
to solve when he became aware that his father,
who sat at his little desk in the corner, was speaking to him, or at least speaking his perplexed
thoughts aloud.

"I'm sure I don't know what to do!" he was saying, and he held in his hand an open letter. "I don't
know how to put off those men, after writing to
them myself and urging their coming."

"What men are they, Father?" David moved toward him with an earnest wish in his heart that he
might in some way be a comfort to that tired, worried man.

Mr. Holman answered almost testily; he was unused to explaining his business matters to anyone.
"Oh, nobody that you know — men who are coming to talk over plans about the south meadow

property. I hoped to accomplish something by
their coming. I've had a hard time working up
their interest and seem to have succeeded. And
now comes an invitation from the largest grape-
grower in Lakeport. He wants me to meet him and
a half-dozen other men day after tomorrow to consult about organizing a society, or a trust, or something of the sort, with a goal of protecting our
interests. Something of that kind ought to be done,
and he's the very man to lead in it. I would like to
be at the conference and get myself counted in. But
I can't do it, for I mustn't be away now of all
times."

David tried to tutor his voice to express nothing
but business interest as he said, "I see the problem.
I wonder if your interests could be represented at
the conference at Lakeport by a third party?"

It had its pitiful side, that look of bewilderment
on his father's face. "Who is there to represent
me?"

"I thought possibly I might do so."

"You!" Mr. Holman wheeled about in his chair
and gazed at his son. "Are you in earnest, David?
Such an idea had never occurred to me. But why
not? You could manage the business better than I
could myself, I daresay. There are technicalities
and points of law to be thought about. Your legal
studies would come in helpful there, if you haven't
forgotten them entirely. It fairly bewilders me,
though. The truth is, I can't get used to the thought
that I have a son to call upon."

David's smile was good to see. "You're accustomed only to a son to wait upon; I'll try to show
you that you have one to serve you. Who is the
man that is to be visited in Lakeport?"

CHAPTER XII

I WILL SEEK HIM WHOM MY SOUL LOVETH

is name is Rothwell," explained Mr. Holman, referring to the letter. "You won't remember him. He's a new man, and the leading man in that part of the country. He has a beautiful place about a mile from town. Why, it's the old Symonds place. You remember that? He's made a paradise of it, I've been told. I don't know the man, except by reputation. But people everywhere seem to have the highest opinion of him, and I like his letter extremely well. It is manly and businesslike and at the same time friendly."

As he spoke, he placed the letter in his son's hand, adding, "Do you really mean that you think you can go? Are you well enough, strong enough?

It seems very strange!"

"I'm perfectly well," said David with his brightest smile, "and it will make me immensely happy to go for you, Father."

His voice was quiet enough, but his heart was in a tumult. How strangely and unexpectedly his way had opened before him! Not only was he being sent to the very city of his desires, but to the very house where he had been told that the new teacher was welcomed and honored. Surely this did not simply "happen." Was the guiding hand of God marking out his way?

The next day was crowded with activities. In the first place, his father's business must be gone over in detail so that no possible question could come up and find him unprepared. This of itself was interesting. The father, unused to explaining his business methods, talked in riddles at first. The son questioned and jotted down items and returned to them and questioned again and finally offered suggestions.

At last his father's troubled face cleared, and he said with a relieved air, "I believe you understand parts of it better than I do myself. What a head you have for business! You can be a rich man yet, David."

Every member of the household was interested. It was an event for David to take a journey.

"What a fuss we are making!" said Margaret, as she tucked a little package into the valise that his mother was carefully packing. "One would think you were going on a pilgrimage!"

"I am," said David. He had a significant smile for Frances, who alone knew the peculiar interest which the trip had for him.

Still, every step of the way was fraught with interest to one who had been so long shut out from the world. To meet and converse with businessmen, as one of them, was like a fulfilled dream of long ago. Undoubtedly these were subordinate interests. He had assured himself, as he trod the streets of the once familiar city, that the central object of his thoughts was gaining more and more of a supreme control of him. For the present he must hold it well in check and put his father's matters first. He was there to transact business for another.

The men who had gathered at Mr. Rothwell's invitation found this young representative keenly alive to the interests that he represented, fairly well posted as to what had been done and pronounced in his ideas of what should be.

A looker-on at David Holman during that busy day would have said that he was absorbed in the grape-growing industry and that he meant to make his mark among businessmen. Yet every nerve in his body was attuned to another interest. He let no word escape him that could throw possible light on the problem he felt he had come there to study. Because of this, it was with peculiar satisfaction that he received and accepted a cordial invitation to return home with Mr. Rothwell when the day was done and spend the night.

This was an entirely unexpected opportunity. He had intended, of course, to stop in town at a hotel. But Mr. Rothwell, who at first glance had drawn him powerfully, was so earnest and hearty in his offer of hospitality that it would almost have been churlish to have declined it. David was only too glad that this was so.

The old Symonds place that had charmed his boyhood was so changed that he could scarcely bring himself to believe it was the same. Cultivated

tastes and evidently ample means with which to
indulge them had wrought marvels. Not that there
was any redundant or even lavish display of
wealth merely as wealth. Nature had simply been
assisted to make the most of her beauty. The house
was nestled in among vines and plants of a semi-
tropical character, as if it were hiding from rude
gaze. Once within its walls, every room repeated
and emphasized the same thought.

Over the door of what was evidently the family
room hung an exquisitely painted motto, the letters of which were composed of branches of cedar
and sprays of fern. The words were:

THE LORD WILL BLESS HIS
PEOPLE WITH PEACE

Not only the motto but the books and papers
lavishly displayed, even a certain something in the
very air itself, seemed to mark this as a home
whose religious life was made a center. David, as
he rested in the easy chair where his host had
placed him after giving due attention to his physical needs, went over in detail the prominent events
of the day. He hoped to discover, if he could, the
subtle spell which Mr. Rothwell seemed to weave
about those with whom he came in contact. All day
it had been marked, and it had been apparent that
others felt the same.

Unquestionably he had been the leader in the
business conference which had just closed and had
shown himself the alert, far-seeing businessman,
quick to make the right suggestion at the right moment and alive to every suggestion from others
that furthered a common interest. Yet through it all
he had seemed to convey the impression that busi-

ness, nevertheless, had with him been relegated to its true place and was emphatically secondary. How did he do it? David found that he could not have put the explanation into words; perhaps it was an atmosphere.

He had just reached the conclusion that if the ladies of this household were in any sense of the word their brother's equals, this must be an ideal home; thereupon the door opened and his host entered, followed by a young woman in the simplest of white dresses, with no other ornament than that which her luxurious hair gave to a singularly pure face. The introduction was very simple: "Mary, let me make you acquainted with Mr. Holman, who will be our guest tonight; my sister, Mr. Holman."

So this was the "rosebud" of whom Miriam Brownlee had told him. He decided instantly that he never would have applied that name to her. Would not "snowdrop" have been more appropriate? No, for that seemed cold, indifferent, and this woman, while very quiet, did not impress one as cold or as centered in self.

I think I should say "lily," the guest mused, carrying on his whimsical comparisons while he outwardly joined in the conversation — unless, indeed, that name is too stately. It is not too pure. I think it fits her.

She stood for a moment in the glow of the setting sun. Her hair, almost a gold color, seemed to flash back the sun's rays, but her face was the very embodiment of purity and peace. Involuntarily David's eyes glanced from her to the motto over the door: "The Lord will bless his people with peace." Unquestionably this was one of His people. She was like her brother; David recognized that from the first moment. He still had to ask him-

self how it was that their belonging to Him was so
evident.

There was also that curious impression, which
the brother had already given him, that these two
had interests of vast importance with which he had
nothing in common. Being an utter stranger, this
was to be expected as a matter of course; yet David
found that it affected him strangely. He could almost have petitioned to be let inside at once into
that charmed atmosphere which pervaded their
lives. Of what or of whom did they remind him?
Could it possibly be of the stranger whose face he
had seen but once?

A striking contrast was also forcing itself to the
front and insisting on claiming thought. Could two
young women be more unalike than Miriam
Brownlee and this young girl? He cut short the
question that followed in this train and took himself sternly to task for allowing his thoughts to run
riot in this fashion. He then gave his mind to the
talk of the hour. It was quiet, commonplace talk.
David would not allow himself to believe he was
still drawing comparisons. In the course of the conversation some of the same books he had discussed
with Miriam came before them. It was curious,
though, that this young woman should have had
almost the same feeling about one author that he
himself had expressed to Frances.

But neither books nor kindred topics of any sort
held his close thought. How should he introduce
the subject about which above all others he was
anxious to learn? Suppose rumor had been entirely
wrong, and this household shrank from the very
mention of the stranger? He could not entertain
that supposition. He had seen him once, and there
had been nothing about him to shock people such

as these. They might disapprove, it is true. But
even in that case they could give reliable informa-
tion.

He tried to arrange a conversation which would
lead up naturally to the subject and ended by asking an abrupt question. "Are you interested in the
street scenes which seem to have become a part of
your city's history, Miss Rothwell?"

"Very deeply interested. Surely you are also?"

Her response came instantly with an evident
quickening of interest. Her last word carried the
inflection of a question, and he replied to it.

"Is that a foregone conclusion? Rather, I mean,
are all people becoming interested?"

"I'm sorry to have to answer no. But you — it is
different with you."

She must have heard of him. Instantly he wondered if Miriam had told her of his cure. If so, how
had she told it? He could not say more until he had
discovered just what she knew or thought, so he
asked another direct question.

"Have you heard my story, Miss Rothwell?"

"I *saw* your story. I was present at that meeting,
when your friends brought you, helpless, on a cot.
Yes, I had heard of you as an utterly helpless and
hopeless man, and I saw you rise and walk away in
all the triumph of perfect health. I had never at that
time seen anything so wonderful. I can never forget it, and I'm certain you cannot wish to."

They were fairly launched at last upon the topic
which was evidently of keenest interest to both.
Miss Rothwell was an enthusiastic talker, and she
found an eager listener in David Holman. Story
after story, each in itself a marvel, flowed from her
lips, glowing with the vividness that came from
her being a sympathetic eyewitness.

"But his deeds, wonderful as they are, are not more faith-inspiring than his words," she said at last. "You should hear one of his talks. I don't know whether to call them sermons or lectures. They seem, when one is present, more like conversation with one's friends. The people don't hesitate to interrupt him to ask questions, and he never acts as if he considered it an interruption."

"Have you ever questioned him, Miss Rothwell?"

"Not in public, but I've often done so in the quiet of our home. He stays with us whenever he comes to the city, or at least whenever he can get away from the crowds. He comes here to rest, and we try not to have him disturbed while with us. He must be in sad need of rest. The people throng and press him all the time. We had hoped he would be with us this week, but he has gone away again without taking any rest."

A summons to the tea table interrupted their conversation, and after tea there seemed to be no good time for renewing it. The talk became general, and Mrs. Symonds, who was very unlike her sister, led and indeed at times monopolized it.

Mary Rothwell slipped quietly away and seated herself alone on the moonlit porch, where David looked out at her wistfully from time to time. He would have been glad of an excuse for joining her. So eager had his heart grown for more talk about the new friend with whom she was so well acquainted that he found it difficult to hold his thoughts in the direction of common conversation. He was glad when their host proposed early retirement, after the fatigues of the day.

As he led the way to the guest chamber, he said, "We are giving you a signal honor tonight, Mr.

Holman. I hope your heart appreciates it. This is the room which our special friend occupies whenever he can get away for a night of rest. We rarely offer it to others; we like to hold it ready for his use at any moment that he may choose to come. But some domestic arrangements or changes have put our guest chamber temporarily out of order; therefore we make you welcome here. We hoped we had reason to believe you would enjoy the room all the better because of its usual occupant."

"I am honored indeed!" said David. His voice was so full of feeling that his host made sure he was not mistaken in his estimate.

Left alone, David threw himself upon a couch that had evidently been prepared for giving as much rest as possible to a weary body. He relished the thought that he was actually sitting where that man was in the habit of resting. He leaned forward presently and touched reverently the rows of books on the well-filled shelves at the end of the couch. He imagined the hands of the stranger touching them. He tried to think how he must look with his face in repose and his thoughts on books and other everyday matters such as filled common lives.

Never in his life had David Holman's heart thrilled with the thought of any person's friendship, as the mere mention of this stranger's name had begun to thrill him. The feeling, instead of quieting with the passing days, was increasing in power. What would be the outcome? Evidently he was the guest of a family who understood such a mental condition and shared it. Indeed, in them it was perhaps intensified, as would be natural with those who knew the stranger well and were indeed privileged to call him their friend.

And yet, mused David, he cannot be to them what he is to me. What is friendship compared with a relationship born of infinite helpfulness? Let me remember what a word, a look, from him did for me. Is it any wonder that I have a feeling of loving reverence for him that amounts almost to worship? Yet that, of course, is wrong and is unlike me. I must hold myself in check. But I must know more about that man. I must understand from him what his power over me is. I must brave my father and Miriam and everybody, if necessary, to know this. It's not possible to be content with less than this. Indeed, after what has passed, I can't think it would be right."

Having reached a decision that he meant should not be altered, he tried to put it all aside and knelt for his evening prayer. But here again was an experience that disturbed, even shocked, him. The image of the stranger came between him and his heavenly Father! It came persistently, refusing to be put aside. He arose at last, shocked and distressed. What did it all mean? Was his mother right in attributing the influence to the great enemy of men? Even if it were reasonable to suppose that the age of prophets had come again, a prophet should not come between a man and his God. That was idolatry!

All things considered, the night was a disturbed one. David's broken sleep was troubled by perplexing, contradictory dreams, and his waking thoughts were hardly less disquieting. Morning found him with only one fixed idea — the determination to seek a personal interview with this master of his thoughts as soon as it was possible to do so.

CHAPTER XIII

HE IS DESPISED
AND REJECTED
OF MEN

Instead of returning home the next day, as he had expected to do, David Holman was detained for several days. The morning mail brought an important letter from his father, who seemed to have awakened to the fact that he had a son who could share his business burdens. He wanted David to call upon several men in the neighboring towns and attend to certain matters of business that had been waiting for some time.

It was, therefore, not until the evening of the fifth day after his departure that David reached home again, to find a state of things that engrossed his time and thoughts.

Word had come from the Brownlees that the

young son and heir was very seriously ill. Margaret had been his playmate in childhood and his daily companion during his schoolboy life and was almost as fond of him as she would have been of a younger brother. She had gone to see what help she could offer to the distracted mother.

"The messenger asked for you," Frances explained, "and said that Mrs. Brownlee would be distressed to hear that you were not at home. That was yesterday morning. We didn't write because we expected you last night, you remember. This morning I had a line from Miriam. John is no better, and she says that he asks constantly for you. He's delirious, I suppose. He doesn't seem to understand that you're away and keeps imploring them to go and bring you."

David arose promptly from the table where he had been taking a hurried supper and announced his intention of going at once to the sick boy. Oh, no, he wasn't tired — not seriously so, at least. He had rested well the night before. "Besides, I'm very strong — remember?" he had replied to his mother's solicitations with a reassuring smile. He would remain through the night at least, probably longer. They must be in need of some man about, besides the servants. He'd return as soon as he could conveniently, because there was so much in the way of business to explain to his father. But a few days' delay would injure nothing.

As he rode slowly up the steep hillside in the gathering darkness, he could not help reflecting on the Providence that seemed to be hedging his path. He had come home strong in the resolve to let not another day pass before he had a talk with his father and explained to him how positively he had decided upon that next step. His ideas of honor

held him from taking it until the father understood, but he had meant for there to be no more
delay. Now here was delay, not of his planning.
Was it an omen? Did it mean that he had been
about to take a step that was wrong? No comfort
was to be gained from reasoning in a circle, and he
tried to dismiss the subject until he could see his
way more clearly.

Upon arriving at the Brownlees', he found an
almost distracted household. Miriam, who had
been so much in her uncle's home that her cousin
John seemed as a brother to her, was scarcely less
distressed than his mother was.

"Oh, David!" she exclaimed, going back to the
familiar name of long ago, as she met him at the
door. "You can't think what a comfort it is to see
you! How could you wait so long? Poor John is
tossing from one side of the bed to the other, calling constantly for you. Not that he knows what he
is saying, poor boy! He's burning with fever. Still,
we thought it might possibly soothe him to see
you, even if he didn't quite recognize you. Auntie
is almost wild with fear. Oh, David! If John dies,
what *shall* we do?"

This was the beginning of days and nights of
anxious watching and waiting, relieved by occa-
sional glimmers of hope of such short duration
that they seemed to serve only to make the anxiety
more intense. Through it all David Holman proved
himself to be a source of strength. After the first
day of watching, he took in the situation, realizing
what a long, hard struggle was before them at the
best. He went home that night, had that important
business talk with his father and put all details as
to what had been accomplished in his hands. He
then made preparations for a long stay on the hill-

top and returned to install himself as head nurse.
He was invaluable during the long night vigils, being the only one who could effectively relieve the
mother.

It took but the experience of one night to prove
his skill as a nurse.

"I haven't been taken care of for years without
learning something of how it is done," he said to
Miriam, when she commented on his deft ways in
the sickroom.

Perhaps he had also learned in the same school
how to judge illness better than those did about
him. From the first he had had very little hope of
the young man's recovery. As the days passed and
what hope there was grew hourly fainter, a strong
and ever-increasing desire developed in David's
heart to summon the new and wonder-working
doctor to this bedside. Yet he saw no way of bring-
ing this to pass. He felt the impossibility of doing
anything so long as the mother clung to a shred of
hope.

As time wore on, and the fever raged with un-
abated persistence, still graver symptoms appeared. The doctors in almost constant attendance
grew more and more reticent. And finally in response to earnest questions they could only sorrowfully shake their heads and speak no word.
David's resolve was made; he would try to urge
the strange physician upon the mother as a last
resort. She could refuse; but at least he would have
relieved his own haunting fear that some deed was
being left undone that might spare the valued life
to them. It was something to have the responsibility shifted. But the task was found to be harder
even than he had imagined it.

Lillian Brownlee had all the violent prejudices of

a weak woman who had trained herself to believe that anything outside of the well-defined, highly respectable road in which the Brownlees and the Brainards, her side of the family, had always traveled was of course very improper, if not radically sinful.

She shuddered and exclaimed and cried over the suggestion. "My dear David! How did you have the courage even to mention such an idea to a Brownlee? Or, even worse, to one who belongs to the Brainards? It frightens me to think what my poor dear father would say of such a course, if he were living. Oh, David, I am very grateful to you for your help, but you *cannot* mean that I should do anything so wild as this! Do you think I would risk offending our family physician and the eminent men he has called in council? They might even leave my dear boy and decline to do anything more for him. It would be a direct insult to them, you know. I could hardly blame them, if I turned to such a source. But, of course, David, you don't mean to urge anything of the kind. I know what it is: You're half distracted, like the rest of us, and hardly know what you are saying. Still, I really think he seems a little brighter this morning, don't you feel so?"

David felt driven to his last resort. "No," he said sorrowfully, "I must speak the truth. I see no improvement. And, dear Mrs. Brownlee, forgive me for such plain words, but I think you should know that the physicians have given up all hope."

The moment the words were spoken he regretted them. Mrs. Brownlee was not the sort of mother who could be roused to definite action by the truth. She lost all self-control. She screamed and groaned and fainted and passed from one pro-

longed fainting turn to another, taxing all the re-
sources of the house. She so alarmed the attending
physician that he said he did not know but the
mother would go first.

In the height of the excitement one doctor in-
sisted upon discovering what had brought on so
violent an attack. Upon close questioning, David
admitted that he had told the mother plainly of the
hopelessness of the case. The doctor asked him
coldly if he did not think she would have discovered it quite soon enough in the natural order of
events.

Poor David, as he turned despairingly away
from the group, felt that a more utter failure could
not have been made. He must give it up, the dear
hope to which he found that he had clung persistently through all those nights of watching. Yet he
did not quite give up. By evening Mrs. Brownlee
had recovered sufficiently to be at her post beside
her son, and he seemed not much weaker than he
had been in the morning.

David resolved to talk to Miriam as though
nothing had been said before. She had great influence with her aunt and so fully realized the hopelessness of the case that she might be ready to catch
at a straw.

He found her in the doorway, where she had
gone for a breath of air, and began without any
preparation. "Miriam" — during those days in
which they shared the watching and anxiety, they
had gone back to the old habits and were David
and Miriam to each other — "Miriam, don't you
think it would be possible to persuade your aunt to
send for the stranger to come and see John? He's in
your own city again, and I could reach him and
return with him by morning. It certainly could do

no harm, and no one can deny the wonderful cures he has performed. Poor John, if he could give his opinion, would be sure to want it. I had a talk with him one day about the man, and he said he wanted nothing so much as to see him for himself."

He was not prepared for Miriam's reception of his words. She turned upon him almost fiercely, her eyes blazing as he had rarely seen them.

"Is it possible," she asked, "that you have been urging such a thing upon my aunt? I understand her illness then. How could you do it? Doesn't she have trouble enough? The idea of thinking that she would insult the physicians whose skill John's life depends upon by sending for that charlatan!"

"Miriam," said David, with sadness and also with a touch of sternness, "why should we play with meaningless words? We both know the doctors have failed. They have no hope. No one who understands sickness has any hope. Do you think sorrow is less difficult to bear because one shuts one's ears to its swiftly approaching footsteps? I was silent as long as — longer than — there remained a shadow of hope that the ordinary means would serve. But now the plain, solemn truth is that John is sinking steadily. Help, if it comes at all, must come very soon. I beg you, Miriam, to put aside prejudice or family pride or anything that stands in the way of making an effort to give him this last chance. Do you realize how little you know of the man to whom you give a contemptuous name? What if he is sent of God to help us all?"

He miscalculated his influence over the angry girl.

She replied with increasing excitement. "You need not use such words with me. I am capable of judging a thing that is before my eyes as well as you are. I know more about this matter than you do. While you have been lying in bed, I have been out in the world, looking on. That man, who has succeeded in deceiving you, has been in our city before. I know what the leading men in town think of him. I know he is more than suspected of designs against the government and that he is using his power over the weak wills of others to work mischief. But he is overextending himself. He'll find that the government is far more powerful than he has imagined. If you think I will lift my finger to help bring that man into my aunt's house, you are greatly mistaken. I should not *dare* to do it. I hope you will believe me in time when I tell you there's danger in this thing. I know what I am talking about."

She paused as if for breath and then went on in tones a shade gentler. "David, I'm not surprised you feel as you do concerning him. In your weak state, you weren't able to realize what time, medicine and good nursing had done for you. And it seemed to you that the man exercised some marvelous power that had to do with your recovery. But it seems very strange that you would think an attack of fever could be cured in the same manner! The David Holman I used to know couldn't have been so easily impressed.

"At all events" — her voice was growing hard again — "the Brownlees decline to be entangled in any such fanaticism. If poor John must die, let him die as he lived and not mix with the rabble. Perhaps he is to be taken away from influences that would ruin him and break his mother's heart. I beg your pardon, David. I know my language sounds too strong. But I know ever so much more about this matter than you think I do. If I could speak more plainly, I would, for the sake of saving you. All I can say now is that to have anything to do with that man or his teaching is dangerous. The time is coming when you will understand and thank me for my warning."

Even after this, David did not utterly despair. It was vain, of course, to hope for Miriam's influence. But he had prayed for help, and what he believed was faith made him cling to a strange feeling that, before it was quite too late, some power would intervene and bring to their aid the one in whom his hopes centered. As the night waned, he asked himself whether, instead of faith, it could be superstition.

Steadily the shadows closed about them. There was a moment of apparent consciousness in which John's eyes roved anxiously from one to another of the group around his bed. He murmured, "David," and David came forward instantly. He bent over the dying face and strove in vain to understand the murmured word. With that beseeching look in his eyes that David thought he could never forget, John Brownlee took the mysterious journey that we name death.

It was David's hand that felt the last convulsive grasp of those white fingers. It was David who did for the lifeless body all those last tender acts that love can perform. After that he went away. Margaret had been in attendance almost as steadily as he had himself; Mrs. Brownlee seemed to cling to her, in memory of her long friendship for John. Others were there, ready and waiting to show all possible attention, so David felt that he could easily be spared. Indeed, in view of what had passed, he felt his absence would be better than his presence, and he longed to be alone.

There was need for him at home. The father had been unexpectedly called away again by urgent business, and his mother was ill. Not alarmingly so — but to have the busy mother, whom everyone in the family leaned upon, sick enough to lie passive during the working hours of the day was strange enough to awaken anxiety.

On the morning after his return home David announced to Frances that he had decided not to attend the funeral. He was not anxious anymore about their mother, for she seemed much better to him; but he believed that course would be the wiser.

Mrs. Brownlee had not seemed to care to talk with him since that morning when he urged upon her what she would not do. Possibly the sight of him now, when it was too late, might arouse unavailing regret that she had not tried even that. He did not wish to make her burden heavier than it already was. There was excuse enough for his absence, with their father away and their mother ill.

So brother and sister remained at home, trying to do their work as usual, and gave themselves to many sad and tender memories of the bright-faced boy who was gone. They had all been fond of him. During his earlier years the two families had been neighbors, and John had felt almost as much at home with them as he had with his father and mother. It was a bitter thought to David that the boy had been allowed to slip out of life without that supreme effort being made to save him upon which his own heart had been set.

CHAPTER XIV

HE HATH SENT ME TO BIND UP THE BROKENHEARTED

"I don't think I understand your feeling," Frances said, when her brother confessed to her that he could not rally from the pain of his bitter disappointment. "It's God's plan that there shall be a time to die. Surely you don't believe he would have allowed John to die before that time came? If you think this stranger would have cured him, or that he can and will cure anybody who is ill, how is God's settled plan to be carried out? Why, David, that idea logically worked out would abolish death!"

"No," said David, "you don't understand. If you'd ever seen the man, you would be sure he would perform no act except in line with the will

141

of God. I don't feel sure that he would have cured
John. It may have been, as you say, God's time for
John to go. I don't believe I can make my meaning
clear to you. It isn't clear enough to me to be for-
mulated. Of one thing I am sure: This man, whoever he is, has special and very close relations with
God, and appealing to him seemed almost like appealing to God Himself. You don't quite get my
thought? No wonder! Never mind. What I felt was
an unconquerable desire to bring him and John together. But I failed, and there's no use in talking
about it now."

He turned from her abruptly, and Frances could
see that he was deeply and strangely moved.

Toward the sunset of that sorrowful day, David
came in from the garden where he had been working and sought Frances in the dining room.

"Something must have happened in town," he
said. "The people passing by are so absorbed in
something that they don't even look toward the
house, and that, you know, has been unusual of
late with our house. A moment ago the Warfields
passed. They were so excited in their talking that
they didn't see or hear me, even though I called
after Joe with the idea of asking what had happened."

"I wish we didn't live in such an isolated place,"
Frances replied. "We never get any news until the
day afterward. This is the least traveled road of
any that leads to the city, but that's no wonder,
when they keep it in the shape they do. I thought
Margaret would come home this evening. Didn't
she say when she would come?"

"Not definitely. There was no opportunity. She
expected us there today, you know. However,
Jonas would bring her down whenever she was

ready to come. But I think they'd keep her at least until tomorrow. They'll be very desolate tonight. Ah, there's Philip! Now we'll hear what all the excitement is about. Political news of some sort, I presume."

Frances went softly to close the door to her mother's room so that she might not be disturbed by the sound of voices, while David turned to welcome their guest. It required only a glance at his face to know that something had moved him powerfully.

"What is it?" David asked before any greetings had been exchanged.

"Haven't you heard anything?" he asked eagerly.

"Nothing whatever. I've been here at home since I came from the Brownlees'. But I was just telling Frances that something had occurred to create quite an excitement. I felt it in the people who passed by. What has happened?"

"When did you come from the Brownlees'? Were you there when John died?"

"Yes — I held his hand during its last clasp. After that I did for him all that could be done and came away. Our mother is ill, and Father is away from home, so Frances and I did not return for the funeral."

"David, are you sure that John Brownlee *died?*"

David's face paled before the intensity of the sentence.

"What a question!" he said. "Didn't I tell you I was with him at the very last and that I prepared his body for the grave?"

"Nevertheless, he is as much alive at this moment as you are, and as full of vigor."

Frances suppressed what would have been a

scream but for David's quick glance toward his mother's door. As it was, her brain reeled, and the room grew dark about her. She had just strength enough left to drop into a chair. Neither of the gentlemen took note of her; they were staring at each other in equally intense excitement.

"What does it mean?" said David at last. "What are we to think or say? What do they think? Did you see him, Philip?"

"I saw him," said Philip, struggling to speak quietly. "I heard him say, 'Mother,' and saw the smile on his face. You don't ask me how it came to pass, David, or who was there."

"I have no need," murmured David.

But Frances, who had rallied from her faintness, pressed in her questions. "Oh, Philip! What happened? Can't there be a mistake? Did you attend the funeral? Oh! Was there a funeral?"

"Begin at the beginning," said David. "How is it that you were there? Did *he* come to attend the funeral?"

"No, we were not to be there. At least I'd heard nothing of such a plan. We were going toward the city, we twelve who have been with him lately. Just as we were passing the bend in the road that leads to the cemetery, we met the procession. I had forgotten about the burial; I mean, that it was to take place this afternoon. You'll think that strange. But...we had had a wonderful day. I was simply absorbed over the things I had heard and seen, so that all less important matters left my mind. When we saw the procession, we halted at a respectful distance to allow it to pass. I stood near him and was watching his face. Just as those who bore the coffin neared us, he stepped forward, laid his hand on the coffin and directed them to halt.

"We were startled and troubled; we know so much! One of our number murmured that it would make him more unpopular than ever to detain a funeral procession and that it was no time to talk to people. Still, he was obeyed. The tone was one that men would not be likely to disregard — not harsh, but commanding. At the same moment he turned to Mrs. Brownlee and in a voice of infinite tenderness said, 'Do not weep.' And then, Frances, David, he bent over the body and said, 'Young man, arise.' "

"What!" said David, springing up. "He spoke to the *dead!*"

"Aye, and the dead *heard!* He used a much quieter tone than I am using now. An indescribable tone — it expressed quiet assurance. Yet there had been no calling upon God, no word of prayer. The instant he spoke, John sat up smiling and said, 'Mother.'

"What followed you must imagine; human language can't describe it. There was of course near hysteria. I had to tend to Margaret, who fainted and had to be carried back to the carriage. I saw him, however, take John's hand and, bending over, place it in his mother's while he spoke a few words intended for her alone. She stood like one transfixed; I don't think she realized at the time that it was John who was speaking to her. The crowd did, however, and it increased every moment. The excitement was overwhelming. We thought he would speak to the people. Instead, he signaled to us to come and instantly moved away. Of course, they followed us for a long distance, shouting themselves hoarse, but he took no note of it."

A moment of intense silence followed. His listeners were too moved for words. At last David repeated the words he had used at first: "What are we to think?"

"I don't know," said Philip, drawing a long breath. But his tone was that of one who recognized a turning point in his career. "That is, I don't understand fully. Indeed, I may say that I understand very little. But this much I am sure of — the man who has come into our midst so silently and yet with such power is not merely a man. He is more even than the prophets were who used to be among us hundreds of years ago. I speak the words reverently and with due consideration of their solemn import. It would take very little to convince me that he is the Christ toward whom all our hopes have been turned."

Frances held herself to perfect silence, but David uttered an exclamation almost of terror. "Oh, Philip! Not that!"

Philip turned to him quickly. "Why not? What is our faith or hope? Don't we believe he is to come? Haven't we been taught to watch for him? Aren't our Scriptures full of the story? Hasn't it been the central pivot of our faith for ages?"

"Ah, that indeed! But there is surely no earthly grandeur great enough for that coming One. This man is poor and obscure and mingles constantly with the common people. Just a few days ago I heard he was reared in a region not far from here. It's said that his parents are very humble people, and he himself has been reared as a carpenter. All of this may not be true, but portions of it are well authenticated. Did you hear these things? How are they to be reconciled with ideas like those you hint at?"

"My friend, if I were not entirely sure that you did not speak those words in the spirit in which I heard them spoken only a few days ago, dear as you are to me, I would cease to call you friend."

"What spirit was that?" David asked, more for gaining time to quiet the strength of his own feeling, and to give Philip a chance to recover himself, than because he thought he cared for the answer.

"I heard Miss Brownlee say with that disdainful laugh of hers, 'Your boasted teacher is a mere carpenter, who worked every day at his trade until his ambition was roused to be a reformer or a public character of some sort. What do you think he proposes to accomplish besides mischief?' The tone was more insulting than the words. I can't describe to you how it stung me. If she hadn't been a woman — "

He checked further speech and struggled with his indignation and his pain.

As for David, he had been silenced; he hadn't expected to hear a quotation from Miriam.

There was silence in the room for several minutes.

Then Philip spoke again, his tone quite changed. "Forgive me, David. I know you don't question me in any such spirit as that. As for me, my spirit is very different from that of the one I'm trying to follow. Let me explain my position, if I can, since we've begun this talk. I don't profess to understand fully, but it's beginning to seem to me that we have been reading our Scriptures with our eyes shut. What can such words as these of the prophet Isaiah mean? 'He is despised and rejected of men; a man of sorrows, and acquainted with grief: and we hid as it were our faces from him; he was despised, and we esteemed him not.' Doesn't that sound like a commentary on the present state of things?

"David, if you were going about the country as I

am and could hear the words of contempt and ridicule poured upon this man who has done only good, and good continually, ever since he came among us, I believe your soul would burn within you, indignant over these wrongs. And I think you would begin to feel with me that perhaps our treatment of him was described hundreds of years ago."

At that moment David heard his mother's voice speaking his name. He went at once to her room, closing the door carefully behind him.

It was Philip Nelson's opportunity. He turned to Frances, speaking hurriedly as one who felt that opportunities were scarce. "Frances, I'm afraid you'll think this an inappropriate time for the words I must speak. The conditions are certainly not as I had planned them. But neither is my life in any way what I had planned, and I don't know what is coming. It's because of this uncertainty that I feel I shouldn't wait for a fitting opportunity.

"I'm sure you know, without a word from me, all that I want to say and have wanted to say for many months. If I hadn't thought you understood me perfectly, I could not have kept silence so long, as hindered as my way has been. It has been my dearest hope to get my affairs so arranged that I could honorably ask your father to give me the right to shield and care for you. The right to love you above all other earthly loves I took long ago. I also think you understand something of what has lately come into my life and changed everything. No, not everything — it has intensified my love for you and my desire to claim you as my own. But the way is more hedged than before.

"To some it will seem as if I had deliberately hedged it, when it was growing less involved. I've given up regular work, as you know. I'm earning almost nothing, and I am under the direct leadership and control of this stranger, who is looked upon with distrust by some and with contempt by many. Oh! It's worse than contempt. He is hated by those in high places, who are dangerous enemies. I fear sometimes that even his life is in danger.

"Yet of my own will I have joined myself to him and made his interests mine. Can you understand such an act? If I thought you couldn't, I would be indeed miserable. But I've hoped, I've believed — what have I believed? Oh, my friend! Do you see how impossible it is for me to say what under other circumstances I could?"

He had hurried out the words as though they must be spoken — and as though he expected every moment to be interrupted. He waited for the girl's reply with an intensity that was almost painful. Surely stranger wooing never was.

Frances still sat in her mother's chair into which she had dropped when the deathly faintness overtook her. Her eyes were so fixed upon him that she seemed to read his very thoughts. The deadly pallor was still upon her face; but she was not excited, and she did not keep him waiting long for a reply.

"This is no time for playing with words, Philip. I will speak as plainly to you as you have to me. I do understand you and have understood for some time. Since you are the man you are, I could do no less. I also think that you understand me; I have not attempted to conceal what you are to me. Why should I? We can pass that part; we understand each other. But the way is hedged, as you say — more thoroughly hedged than ever before.

"You know my father, you think. But I know him better. His prejudices are part of his life. Once let them get firm hold, and nothing human can affect them. I almost said that neither could anything divine. I know he's a man of prayer. But I've seen him rise from his knees with exactly the same feelings he had when he knelt — when from my standpoint it would have been impossible to have harbored such feelings and pray at all.

"Against this stranger, who has become so much to you, my father's prejudices have been roused as I've never seen them before. The feeling grows upon him. He is more severe in his judgments and stern in his commands with each passing day. I dread the time when you will be forbidden in the house because you call yourself that man's friend."

Philip interrupted her. "I know, Frances. I've seen more of the feeling than you think. But it can't last. It's impossible for such a man to nurse prejudice in view of such a stupendous deed as has been performed this day. Think of it — a dead man raised to life and vitality by a word! And his voice as he spoke to the mother, telling her not to weep — I wish I could tell you how it sounded! Do you know what I thought of? 'He hath sent me to bind up the brokenhearted.' Do you remember the connection? Does it sound like blasphemy to you, or do you — oh, Frances! Tell me you understand my thought and are in sympathy with it!"

CHAPTER XV

A MAN'S HEART
DEVISETH HIS WAY

 understand what you mean," she said with exceeding gravity. "As to what I think, I'm trying to hold my judgment in abeyance. I don't need to tell you which way my heart prompts. But, Philip, let's look matters plainly in the face and not deceive ourselves. This feeling or belief of yours widens the gulf between us immeasurably. I have no hope from this new act, wonderful as it is.

"I know my father. When David came home well, I was wild with hope. I felt sure that Father and Mother would at least be convinced that here was a subject for careful investigation. But you saw how it was. My father had been with David day and night for years. He knew just how powerless he was and also how impatient; several times he had injured himself almost past rallying in trying to exercise willpower. And yet he has allowed himself to absorb Felix Masters's theory and now talks freely about the wonderful power of mind over matter, citing David as an illustration! If I hadn't heard him myself, I couldn't believe my father could be so deluded. After that, what is there to hope for?"

"Still," persisted Philip, "the cases are different. I know there's a great deal of such talk as Masters puts forth. One wonders whether he can really believe what he says. But it will be simply impossible to argue against an actual return to life! I can only believe that we have an event now that will make honest people stop and think and study their Scriptures as they never have before."

Frances shook her head. "Nothing will make some people think on subjects they don't want to think about," she said sadly. "Remember Mr. Masters. I haven't the least idea that he believes in himself. He's the governor's nephew, though, and a powerful enemy where he chooses to be. The more I see of him, the more sure I am that there is a definite purpose hiding behind all his bitterness. And he has great influence over my father."

"And you will not brave your father? Is that what you mean?"

"I must not, Philip. I know only just enough to be sure that that would not be right."

"Tell me one thing, Frances. How does my conduct seem to you? Am I wrong? Should I leave this man and return to my work and thereby appease my own father, whose indignation against me has no bounds? If I do that, I can plan in time for our home together."

A faint smile hovered over her face as she said, "You can't do it, Philip. He has shown you his way. You *must* follow him. Besides, you think it would be wrong, and you cannot do wrong. Philip, will you answer one question? Has this man asked you to follow him literally, about the country, wherever he goes?"

"Yes, definitely."

"Then...I have come just so far as this. If I were you, I would obey him literally, no matter what he asked, until I had received further light."

A flash of joy illumined Philip's face; but what he would have said in reply will not be known, for at that moment David returned, and very soon thereafter the caller went away.

The next morning brought Margaret, but she was in a very nervous, restless state. The eager questions of the family seemed to stir up in her an unreasoning irritability.

"Of course it's all true!" she said. "You don't think, I suppose, that Philip trumped up the story for your entertainment!"

"John? To be sure I saw him. He came to breakfast this morning."

"Certainly he's well — never looked or acted better."

"Oh, as if I could tell you how they feel! Mrs. Brownlee is simply insane with delight. I scarcely saw her, though. They're trying to keep her quiet in her room; the doctor says she's too excited. John stays with her most of the time. The program has been changed; now he's taking care of her."

"Why, Frances, of course I saw it all. What strange questions you ask! I was directly behind Mrs. Brownlee and Miriam. I couldn't avoid very well seeing all that took place."

A little later, in response to David's question, she said, almost angrily, that she did not see how she could be expected to tell her impression of the stranger. It was not a time for one to study impressions; it was simply a scene of the wildest excitement. If they had been there, they would understand how impossible it was to talk about it.

Nothing was plainer than the fact that Margaret's nervous system had received such a shock that she could not control herself. It was David who first realized this and who tried to turn the talk into other channels. But in his heart he was deeply disappointed. He had looked forward eagerly to Margaret's coming. He had not believed that a young, unprejudiced nature like hers could come in contact with that winning stranger under such circumstances and not be powerfully drawn toward him.

He spoke of it to Frances afterward. Wasn't she surprised and disappointed? He had thought that Margaret, with her impetuous nature and warm heart, would respond quickly to the charm of the stranger's manner.

"No," said Frances gravely, "I'm not surprised. I didn't expect an unbiased judgment from Margaret. Our sister has become merely an echo. She reflects what Felix Masters thinks, or rather, what he says. If that man had never entered our home, David, the chances for us all to have happiness, or at least peace, would be better."

As David thought over this last conversation, he drew a little crumb of comfort from it. The elder sister had furnished a clue to Margaret's strange and disappointing state of mind. The child was not herself anymore. She had seen with the eyes of Felix Masters and heard with his ears.

It would be different with Miriam Brownlee. No one who exercised marked influence over her was violently prejudiced against the stranger; at least he persuaded himself that such was the case. Her aunt, it is true, would be prejudiced against anything outside of conventional lines. But it was Miriam who generally influenced her aunt; Miriam's was evidently the stronger nature. He could remember the time when his opinions had power to sway her. Once it might almost have been said of her as he had said of Margaret that she saw with his eyes and heard with his ears.

Wasn't it possible that something of this influence still remained, notwithstanding his recent effort and failure? She had been under such a prolonged mental strain at that time that it was not fair to judge her by that experience. Probably she was not even aware that her language and manner had been so violent. Moreover, young women did not always reveal how much they were swayed by others. His words to her that night might even have prepared the way for what followed.

Certainly by this time she must have a very different feeling for the man who had come into such wonderful relations with the family. If his kind, serious eyes had rested upon her but for a moment, David believed that she must have felt their power.

The more he went over the recent past in the light of the explanations he had made, the more fully did the spell of other days weave itself about him once more. Miriam had once been the embodiment of all that was fair and lovely; she must be still. What if she had said reckless words on that one evening he had spent with her? He remembered that in the long ago she would sometimes take on a mood of daring frolic and delight in shocking staid and dignified people just a little. Often he had listened with scarcely veiled amusement to a sharp war of words between her and some pronounced caller, knowing all the while that there was no such radical difference of opinion between them as Miriam was trying to make appear.

Why mightn't some such mood have possessed her on the evening in question? She might have felt that he, of all others, would be sure to understand her. Was it not reasonable to suppose that she was true to their youthful friendship still? Otherwise, why had she never married? Men high in position and beyond reproach in every way had been her friends. She was not a girl to remain unsought.

By the evening of the second day following John Brownlee's restoration, David had settled all troublesome questions satisfactorily and had resolved to call upon Miriam and, if possible, bridge that gulf of years stretching between them. He was ready to construct a bridge on which they could walk hopefully together, planning their future.

He had been inexpressibly jarred by her, but he assured himself that he had been unreasonable. His coming to her as he did must have in itself seemed almost like a resurrection. Probably it stirred her excitable nature to its depths; he should not have expected her to be her natural self.

Those irritable words she had spoken later, when John was dying, he resolved to ignore altogether; all that was changed now. Miriam had seen and heard for herself.

Nevertheless, he did not make his call at the Brownlees' for several days. His father returned that night with certain business perplexities weighing so much upon him that he seemed to have no ears for the wonders that the neighborhood was athrob over.

He began at once to try to explain matters to his son, relieved immensely by the fact that David lent himself to the subject and promptly showed his grasp of the situation.

"I tell you what, David," he said, after a long conference, during which David had more than once offered suggestions that cleared the way. "You certainly have a better head for business than I ever had. You will make a success of it. I have been able only to keep my head above water. I could almost wish you had lost your interest in the law and were willing to take hold with me and make these plans come to what you see in them. I feel that you could do it, and I'm afraid that I can't.

"Still, of course, I do not want to tie you down to a life that you have not chosen for yourself. You will make a successful lawyer, without doubt, and be able by your advice to tide me over dangerous places, I daresay.

"This much, though, I wish you would do for me. Can you go in my place tomorrow and settle all the complications of this business? You could do it much better than I. Your knowledge of legal terms helps wonderfully, and you see into what people mean quicker than I do. Also, you can express what you think briefly and intelligently, which is more than your father ever succeeds in doing. Besides, to tell the truth, I am tired out and a little worried about your mother. I'm not used to seeing her in bed. It does not seem as though I could start off again tomorrow."

David's first thought was of Miriam Brownlee. He had told himself emphatically only an hour or

two earlier that tomorrow evening he would go to
her. His second thought was for the man he hoped
to meet somewhere very soon, just as soon as he
had had that talk with Miriam and also with his
father. The latter seemed necessary to him, or, at
least, it was the honorable course. Still, these matters were strictly personal.

Should his father's interests suffer while he
cared for himself? He could think more rapidly
than his thoughts can be written, and there was no
perceptible distance between the father's appeal
and the son's reply. Certainly he would go in his
father's stead. He believed he understood the main
facts, and they could go over the details again between now and train time in the morning. He saw
the need for haste in the matter, and of course his
father ought not to go away again so soon.

As it happened, the two or three days that father
and son had believed the business would consume
extended over a period of more than two weeks.
Numberless were the unexpected delays and business complications, involving trips to this and that
town and conferences with persons who had not
been considered in the original plan.

But when at last David swung himself from the
incoming train one early morning and prepared
for a rapid walk out to his home, it was with a
comfortable sense of not only having accomplished in a satisfactory manner the business upon
which he had been sent, but of having several
pleasant surprises for his father. He had been able
to make far better arrangements than either of
them had supposed possible.

The world looked beautiful to him that summer
morning, and life stretched itself out before him as
a joyous thing. He had done much thinking during

his absence about other matters than his father's business. He had gone over his own future, and, as far as a man could, who knew nothing about it, had mapped it out. He had linked it closely with the future of Miriam Brownlee. Once more he had decided that their lives were to flow together as one. Miriam had waited all these years; it must be because she understood her own heart and his. Concerning the other question, he was also in a degree settled. He and Miriam together would investigate thoroughly and dispassionately the entire matter.

He himself had been extreme, perhaps; Philip was extreme and was inclined to be a visionary. He would not distress or prejudice Miriam in any such ways. He would be patient and wait for her growing interest. What these two weeks with her cousin John beside her once more in the glow of health have done toward developing her interest in the subject they were to investigate! He believed she would be ready for him. It was not as though these things were being done in a corner. Everybody must investigate; it was childish folly to do otherwise.

Wherever he had been, the fame of the mysterious stranger had preceded him. He had met many who had come into personal contact with the man and who daily bore about with them glad marks of his power. He had met some who had sneered; this was to be expected. Almost without exception, however, they had been men who held low views of life and duty; who had false conceptions of the Scriptures and their teachings; or who were indifferent to it altogether and ignorant of it. Also they had been chiefly men who were interested only in political questions. These, he had found, looked upon the stranger as an intriguer who had a deep-laid scheme for usurping power.

David felt that he could afford to smile over these, as men who were frightened by their own shadows. Could any man who was really working up a powerful following have been in his right mind and gone about it as this stranger had? The small number of his chosen friends and the commonness of their lives excluded such an idea. Whatever had been quoted from a reliable source as having come from his lips excluded such a thought. Whoever or whatever he was, it would certainly seem as if sane people must agree that he had done not one act to cause alarm and that his entire character and bearing were such as to give him the right to testify for himself.

"And to be believed," David concluded his mental survey aloud with this emphatic thought. "I have gone over the ground a hundred times and find that I always come back to the point that Frances reached by intuition — to believe implicitly what he says of himself, without regard to what others say. To this end I must see him. I wonder what will hinder my way next? If I were superstitious, I might conclude that neither of my two distinctly resolved-upon courses of action was destined to be."

CHAPTER XVI

CAN GOD FURNISH A TABLE IN THE WILDERNESS?

aking a shortcut through the outskirts of the town, David came suddenly upon Philip Nelson resting under the shadow of a stone wall. They exchanged warm greetings, and David inquired half anxiously about his own home. No letters had reached him for several days.

"They're quite well, I think," said Philip. "At least your mother is in her accustomed seat. I was there last evening. Margaret is the least well of any of them, I'd say. Oh, she's not ill — does not call herself so — but she looks far from well. Her eyes have an unnatural brilliancy that I don't like. Frances thinks her nerves have received too great a shock."

"I'm afraid they have," said David gravely. "Do you know if Masters still continues to call at our house?"

"He was there last evening, and I have the impression that he calls quite as frequently as usual. Have you all confidence in that young man, David?"

"I know almost nothing about him. If you mean, am I personally drawn toward him, I am not. Still I know nothing against his character. My father seems to have faith in him."

"I wish I had," Philip said, "for Margaret's sake. But I'm like you — I have no definite charges to make. What have you seen and heard, my friend, concerning the all-important matter, since you've been away?"

"What is the 'all-important matter'?" David asked, smiling. He could not keep his own thoughts away from Miriam Brownlee.

But Philip Nelson's face kept its serious, preoccupied look. "I'm coming to feel that there is but one. You must have heard much about our teacher. His fame is spreading everywhere. It seems strange that you haven't yet come into personal contact with him."

"I haven't, except once. But, as you say, one hears about him continually. And what I have heard has deepened my interest. Is there anything new?"

"Everything is new," said Philip with a faraway look in his eyes. "Every day shows us new truths, new wonders, new power. If you'd only been with us yesterday! We went into the country for a day of rest. At least that was what we thought. It proved to be anything but rest for him. By some means our plans became known to the crowd, and they followed us. The throngs were simply amazing. Men, women and children, hundreds of them, thousands of them! They welcomed us when we went ashore. We crossed to the other side of the lake; it's a very quiet, restful point over there, you know. Very few people seem to have found it out, until yesterday — but I've never before seen such throngs as those that swarmed us all day long. We thought he would go away. But instead he stayed all day, talking with groups of people or speaking to as many in the crowd as his voice could reach. An open-air service — but a service as was never held on this earth before.

"David, there were people there who have gone about for years, bent double with disease. There were lame people and deaf people and those who you and I know were born blind. He cured every one who asked for help. Think of it! Men who had hobbled there on crutches threw them away and shouted and ran! You remember that man with the helpless arm? He was there. I saw him swinging both arms high in the air and shouting himself hoarse for joy.

"There is no use in trying to describe such a scene, but I feel as if you could appreciate it better than others. There were so *many* of them! I'd never seen so much suffering represented in a crowd before. They must have followed him for the express purpose of testing his power — those who had heard the stories, you know. He has a multitude of witnesses now who can give personal testimony.

"That wasn't all. It grew late in the afternoon, and the throngs were pressing him as eagerly as ever. Some of us became anxious as to what was to be done next. We had taken no luncheon with us. I thought that toward afternoon we would go to one

of those villages over there and get food and perhaps spend the night. But there was no indication
that such was his plan. We thought he ought to
dismiss the congregation and advise the people to
go home. Some of them must have come long dis-
tances, and there had been no eating, so far as we
could see, through the day. It had simply been an
unpremeditated rush after the worker of wonders,
without thought of food or of night, and he seemed
to be staying on with them in much the same spirit.
After talking it over among ourselves, we decided
to speak to him and suggest that they be sent home
for food and rest.

"What do you think he said? 'They need not go
away for food; give them something to eat.' David,
I thought I knew the man, but I confess that that
bewildered me. What did he mean? He knew, for
we had spoken of it, that we had taken no food
even for ourselves.

"It occurred to me that perhaps he wanted us to
go to the village and buy bread. That would do for
us. But think of feeding that crowd! Of course we
couldn't do it. I tried to make a mental calculation
and decided that it would take more money than
we were all worth, besides the foolishness of expecting any of those country villages to be prepared for such an onset!

"Still I asked if that was what he meant. He replied by asking if there were any among the crowd
who had brought food.

"Somebody had seen that little lame Jimmie,
who lives at the foot of the mountain, you know,
with a basket of luncheon. He had been too busy
rejoicing over the fact that he wasn't lame anymore
to think of eating, so he had it just as it came from
home — five little rolls and two small dried fishes.

The supply was so absurdly inadequate to the demand that I laughed when I reported it.

"But consider my bewilderment over his reply: 'Seat the people in some sort of order, in groups of fifties, so you can pass among them.'

"Think of our trying to execute such commands as those, with that crowd to manage!

" 'What do you want us to sit down for?' came from all sides. The most we could say was that we were under orders. There was much laughing and exclaiming and endless questions. But that it could be done at all shows what power he has over the crowds. They seemed willing to do whatever he said. I'll tell you who helped us splendidly, David — John Brownlee.

"He moved rapidly among the throngs and seemed to be everywhere, his voice eager and ringing. 'Do just as he tells you, whatever it is. No one will ever regret it.' They couldn't resist him, you know. They had heard his story. In a surprisingly short time the order had been obeyed, and the expected crowd was seated. Then he called for the little fellow's bread and fish and, dividing them among us, sent us out to feed five thousand people!"

"Is it possible?" exclaimed David Holman. His voice expressed more than astonishment. There was awe in it.

Philip felt the tone, and his own grew solemn. "I shall never be able to tell you how I felt when I took that bit of bread in my hand. It was only a mouthful; a child would have eaten it all and cried for more. Could I go to a company of waiting hundreds and offer it as food? Yet I had entered into a solemn pact with myself to follow this man wherever he led — to obey implicitly whatever commands he gave, whether they seemed heavenly wisdom or folly. If he had told me to step into the lake and walk across it to the town in search of food, I would have made the attempt.

"I honestly don't know how to complete my story. Words seem inadequate. I don't know how it came to pass. I know I offered my bit of bread to the first man I reached. He took it and broke some from it and returned it. He had as much as he wanted, and there was more for the next one and the next and the next! Does that sound like the rantings of a wild man, David? It is a solemn fact.

"Nothing he has ever done has impressed me with his power so much as that simple act of creation did. I don't know that I can make the reason plain. But when the helpless leap up and walk, and the dead speak, there is an excitement about the act itself that holds part of a person's attention. But that quiet exercise of creative power, without noise or visible effort of any kind, spoke to me with a voice that I hadn't heard before. Do you remember who it was in our historic past that 'gavest them bread from heaven for their hunger'?

"The marvel went on before our eyes, until every person in that vast throng was entirely satisfied with food. As the scene progressed, the picture grew. An artist who could reproduce it would immortalize himself. When the meal began, the faces of some plainly held sneers, and good-natured jokes and laughter abounded. Only a few faces wore expectant looks, and these, I think, were not expecting bread; the look meant soul-hunger.

"Can you imagine the changes of expression as the hands were held out for bread and received and more applied and were satisfied? No, you can't imagine it. It baffles all description. I tell you,

you must *see the man* in order to understand. Still, I
can give you facts. You have my word of honor that
every man, woman and child in that company
were fed until they could receive no more.

"The added touch was so wonderful. 'Gather up
the fragments,' said our host. Fragments! After
such a meal! Yet each of us filled a basket full of
broken pieces!

"David, I can't think that any sane man, studying him carefully and studying the Scriptures, can
doubt who our leader is! 'And a man shall be as a
hiding place from the wind, and a covert from the
tempest;...as the shadow of a great rock in a weary
land.' " He quoted the familiar words from the
prophet Isaiah with a triumphant smile and a significant glance toward the wall of rock that threw
its welcome shadow over the spot where they were
resting.

David turned anxious eyes upon him.

"But there were miracles performed of old," he
said. "The prophets furnished food in a miraculous
manner; they even raised the dead. I don't see
why, because of such work, one should jump to
such a startling conclusion as yours."

"Perhaps one shouldn't. I'm simply telling you
how I've been impressed. Yes, miracles were performed, but can you recall one in which the power
of God was not invoked? This man commands,
and the helpless and deaf — yes, even the dead —
obey him. When one is present to see these marvels, instead of hearing about them, the effect is
different. I wish, my friend, that you could break
away from the influences that trammel you and
come and be one of us for awhile. I know your
heart is there. Why don't you study the problem in
the best of all ways?"

"There are serious obstacles in my way," David answered with exceeding gravity. "I must think of my father. He's growing old, and I've been a steady weight upon him for years. I mustn't hurt him more than I can help. But you're right in estimating the interest I have, and it's a question that must soon be decided. I'm not exactly halting between two opinions, dear friend. If I *must* grieve others, why, then, I must."

Philip returned no answer. It was not David's father whose influence he feared for him, but he felt that it would be intrusive to speak first of any other.

The world was aglow with moonlight when David Holman started upon that long-delayed errand to the Brownlee home. As he neared the house, the importance of his errand grew upon him. He told himself that if Miriam was not in, he could hardly endure the disappointment. He had waited so long!

As he came in sight of that lovely moonlit piazza and saw the flutter of white garments, he felt his pulses thrill with joy and hope. He had vivid memories of other moonlit nights in which Miriam, all in white, had sat in that very corner waiting for him. It was delightful that she was quite alone.

"Do you know that you're an immense relief?" she said, as she came down the steps to welcome him. "I've been sitting here for the last half hour, watching for John and Auntie. When I saw that the carriage winding up the hill contained but one person, I knew it couldn't be Auntie's carriage. I was afraid it belonged to — well, to someone else." Her soft laugh flowed out, quite as he remembered it.

"The sentence is ambiguous," said David. "But

if I'm not 'someone else,' and you have discovered it, may I hope you are not sorry that it is I?"

The reply was quick and graceful. "Were your friends ever other than glad to see you? We have waited long for your congratulations."

"You know that I've been absent from home?" he asked quickly. "Nothing but necessity has kept me away for so long. Why, I haven't even seen John! And I thought to see him without fail that very next day."

"John is quite well," said Miss Brownlee lightly, "and extremely full of energy — almost too much so. He exhausts us. He and Auntie drove to town several hours ago. I'm expecting their return any moment. Shall we go inside, or will you enjoy the moonlit piazza as I remember you used to?"

"Let's stay here by all means if it pleases you," he said with a quickening of his pulses over those suggestive words. Certainly she remembered their past.

"I like the moonlight on this particular piazza even better than I used to," he said, as he took the seat beside her. And the years that had rolled between them since he last sat there seemed to him as a dream.

The trailing vines with their faint, delicate odor were as they used to be, and the same old moon looked down upon them. The young man believed that his own heart and that of the woman beside him were the same. It seemed to be the most natural thing in the world to speak of those other days.

"Do you remember how we used to sit in this very corner and talk?"

"Do I remember!" The feeling that she threw into those three words almost startled him. All the loneliness of the long years between seemed to sound in them. They hurried him on to speak the words of which his heart was full.

Why should one try to tell the old story? It has been repeated so many times that it is new only to the actors, and it seems just that they should have it to themselves. Let it suffice to say that the young man had no difficulty in making his meaning very plain and that, before they were interrupted, it had been settled that they were to spend their lives together. Not that they tried to plan their future; there was not time for that. Besides, they seemed to like to linger in the past. They made mutual confessions of long, lonely days and years, during which they had desired only each other.

"Let's not allow anything ever to separate us again," murmured Miriam. The slight shudder that ran through her frame might have been from a memory of the past.

David drew her to him, wrapped the fleecy white shawl she wore more closely about her and answered solemnly, "No, never again! Nothing but death can separate us, Miriam. And even death is powerless, except for a little while."

CHAPTER XVII

THEY HAVE TAUGHT THEIR TONGUE TO SPEAK LIES

hen he had thought to tell her immediately of his glad new life which flowed into his soul even before physical strength came to him, determining him henceforth to live for God. He was sure the news would be received joyfully.

In the years gone by, Miriam had often spoken an earnest little word to him that he had always warded off — sometimes with tender merriment, sometimes with a sentimental half promise, forgotten almost as soon as it was made. Miriam had been far ahead of him in those days; he had a happy surprise for her. There did not need to be any divided lives for them. There should be on this

171

subject, as on all others of importance, oneness of thought and purpose.

But there was no opportunity for these revelations. John Brownlee's carriage interrupted them, and it was followed closely by another carriage with four occupants.

"Oh, dear!" exclaimed Miriam. "We're going to have calls. I feared it. This moonlight is so enticing tonight that I felt sure we would be used as an excuse for a drive. Who can it be? Isn't that your sister Margaret's voice replying to Auntie?"

"Yes," said David, rising, "Margaret is on the front seat with Mr. Masters. I don't recognize the others. We shall have no opportunity for further talk tonight, Miriam."

"No," she answered with a little sigh that ended in a laugh. "That sounds hospitable, does it not? I don't always feel so averse to seeing my friends. But I'm sure there's no hope for us; people make such long calls in the country. Never mind, dear, the years will be filled with evenings, just for us."

With the glow of that last word in his heart, he went down to assist the ladies.

"Oh, David!" said John Brownlee, springing to the ground and grasping David's hand in one of his while with the other he held the reins.

"Take care, John!" said his mother. "Selma doesn't like such treatment as that. Look after your horse. David will wait."

"I have been in such haste to see you!" said John. "Selma is all right, Mother. She knows her master. David, when did you get home? I've been down to see you twice. I'm impatient for a talk with you."

"And his mother wants a talk with you, before John has a chance," said Mrs. Brownlee, as they stood waiting for the other carriage, while John led

Selma out of the way. "You're so much older than my dear boy, Mr. Holman, and have so much influence over him that I look to you to steady his impulses. If he should wander off in the direction in which he is now tempted, I think it would break his mother's heart. He's a natural enthusiast, you know. Being so young, it isn't strange that enthusiasm should mislead him. He sadly needs a father's counsel. But the help of an older brother, who is wise and well poised, would be an immense relief. He looks upon you almost as a brother. I know you'll try to help me, David, and not indulge him in ideas that are offensive to his mother. I'm sorry I don't have an opportunity to speak plainer, but perhaps I've said enough to put you on your guard."

As David turned to help his sister Margaret from the carriage, he felt that he understood Mrs. Brownlee very well indeed.

"You're here!" said Margaret. "Frances should have come, and we could've had a family gathering."

The others were introduced as Miss Masters and her friend, Mr. Compton.

The piazza was deserted. No better place could be found for two, but to a lively company of half a dozen, the brightly lighted parlor offered greater attractions. To the merry conversation which at once began, David Holman found himself listening curiously, almost wonderingly. How cheerful they were! What utter nonsense they talked! Life had for years been such a serious matter to him. The days had all been tinged with the reasonable probability that each might be the last on earth that he had to a degree forgotten how full of triviality the average social talk is.

His sister Margaret seemed in her element, the brightest of the bright. He could not help but note that she used a half-mocking tone in speaking to him, as though he lived outside the circle to which she belonged and was of another world than theirs. Indeed, the entire party appeared to look upon him as one who could be expected only to tolerate their fun, not join in it. Yet they admitted Miriam with glee at once into the center of their talk.

As he listened and tried occasionally to join in, David wondered if their estimate were not correct, and he was indeed an outsider. He had not kept himself posted as to the activities of the social world. But he had not guessed that his sister Margaret knew much about the world. If her knowledge came through Felix Masters, she must have been an apt pupil. She seemed to be quite at home on all topics that came up for discussion and, indeed, often led the conversation.

Of course, Miriam was at home in all society matters. He must expect that; her life had been such as to require it. It did not, however, follow that such a life was to her taste. Now that she had admitted him to the first place in her heart, many things would be different. He listened critically to every word she spoke and made constant allowances for any that jarred. And he assured himself that she did not seem as worldly, after all, as did his sister, who had been shielded all her life.

It became increasingly evident that Margaret was indeed learning to see with the eyes of Mr. Masters and to think his thoughts.

Presently David became keenly alert to the fact that the conversation had drifted to the one topic which he had hoped would not be touched that night. He felt how utterly out of accord with the subject this company would be. And he shrank from having Miriam hear more concerning it, until he could have opportunity to set matters before her in their true light. He would not admit to himself that he dreaded to hear words from her lips that would jolt his sensitive nerves.

Yet apparently no instinct told her from what he shrank. It was she who replied to the question from Mr. Masters as to whether they had heard of the latest sensation.

"Indeed we have! You needn't think we live out of the world, because we are on a hilltop. Do you mean the mammoth picnic? How many participated in it today? The last I heard it was six or eight thousand. But it was reported by some to be fifty thousand. Isn't it astonishing how those stories increase in magnitude?"

"Oh, no," said Mr. Masters, "not at all strange — history is simply repeating itself. Gaping crowds have been swarming after something new, with open eyes and mouths, ever since the world was peopled. An exaggeration was ever their trademark."

How light and sweet Miriam's laugh was! " 'Open mouths' is a phrase that exactly fits the situation, Mr. Masters. Was it used advisedly? Who wouldn't open his mouth wide to be fed in so mysterious a manner? It's far superior to the way the poor birds get their living, I'm sure."

"Pray enlighten us," said Mr. Compton. "I don't think that Miss Masters and I have the slightest idea what you're talking about. Have there been any remarkable demonstrations in the line of picnics lately?"

"Oh, I've heard about the picnic," said Miss

Masters, with a cheery little laugh. "Felix tries to
keep me informed, but I pay very little attention to
these matters. I'll have to confess that I never was
deeply interested in the common people. They always have some craze or other to excite them. I
don't understand why so many comparatively respectable people interest themselves in this
strange man and his performances. Why don't
they let the rabble have peaceable possession of
him and enjoy their nine days' wonder, as they
have before?"

"Because this is a very different excitement from
the ordinary," said Felix Masters. His face was
dark and frowning. "The man is very sharp. He's a
keen observer, a student of human nature, and, in
a certain sense, wise. Unless I'm greatly mistaken,
we shall have reason to regret that we allowed him
to get such a hold on the rabble before taking the
matter in hand."

"I insist upon hearing about the picnic," said Mr.
Compton in the tone of one who felt that the conversation might be growing too serious. "Miss
Masters and I extended our ride this morning beyond the limits of civilization and nearly starved
before we reached a point where we could obtain
refreshments. So we're in sympathy with the starv-
ing multitude, if such they were, and in a condition
to appreciate deliverance, if such they had. Give us
the story, please, Miss Brownlee."

"I?" said Miriam brightly. "Oh, it should be
someone who has more dramatic talent than I! Do
you know about it, Margaret? You're just the one to
describe the scene."

Margaret shook her head. "I live in the back-
woods," she said, "and David has been away from
home. I don't hear of wonders until afterward.

What has happened?"

"Why, the story goes," began Miriam, "that the other day 'the rabble' — which is Mr. Masters's name for them, not mine — followed their mysterious leader to an out-of-the-way place and persisted in keeping him company all day. What he did to hold their attention, I'm sure I don't know. 'Talked,' one of them said, and told them 'wonderful things.' Imagine a man talking 'wonderful things' to that class of people!

"However it was, what with the delights of the country and the pleasure of escaping work all day with the 'talk' thrown in, they contrived to stay — dinnerless and, as the day drew near its close, apparently supperless. Some compassionate creature began to wonder what was to become of them before they reached home. In truth, the probability was, I suppose, that most of them wouldn't find much to eat when they did get home. That class of people is not specially provident at any time; the passing moment seems to be all that they think about."

"They're very much like the other class of society in that respect," laughed Mrs. Brownlee. "I've noticed that you young people generally arrange for the present hour without regard to the effect it will have on tomorrow."

Miriam gave her aunt's hand a loving little admonitory pat as she said, "Now, Auntie, please don't moralize. This story has no moral. It's for entertainment, and I want to finish it. Where was I? Oh, they were hungry, all those people — thousands of them, a hundred thousand, if you choose — numbers didn't seem to make any difference. The only provident one among them seems to have been a little fellow who had half a dozen rolls and a dried fish or two. He planned systematically, you see, for a day's pleasure and took his lunch with him like a sensible boy.

"Now comes the remarkable part of the story. That little fellow's lunch was seized upon — or he was petitioned to present it — I'm not up on the details. By some management the rolls were placed in the hands of this wonderful teacher or preacher or whatever name should be his. What did he do but divide them into twelve portions and give them out to his followers, with orders to pass them around the crowd!"

Bursts of laughter followed. Miriam, apparently stimulated thereby, continued briskly: "Oh, you needn't laugh! Cheering would be more appropriate. I want you to understand that every man, woman and child were fed from those rolls! More than that, they gathered up, I won't pretend to say how many, basketsful of food when the meal was over."

The laughter that followed was hilarious. When Mr. Compton could be heard, he asked: "But do the people really believe such stories? How can their credulity be equal to such a strain?"

Standing a little in the shadow near the mantel with his arm resting upon it was John Brownlee. He had not joined in the conversation. No one, unless it may have been his mother, noticed him. She may have observed that he did not smile throughout the recital and that his bright brown eyes flashed ominously.

Suddenly he dashed into the conversation by a question: "Excuse me, sir, but just what do you mean by 'their credulity'? If you had been one of the 'rabble' on that day, if you will allow me to ask you to stretch your imagination to such a degree, would you consider yourself open to the charge of credulity because you believed what you saw and experienced?"

Mr. Compton turned toward him graciously, condescension in his voice and manner. "I might not understand the word, my dear friend, but I think you would be perfectly justified in using it. Of course, that's provided I really believed I had been fed with several thousand others in the manner which has been described."

"Well, sir, how would you account for it? If you had been a spectator and had seen thousands of people eating as much as they wanted and had watched the gathering up of basketsful of food that remained, what would you have concluded?"

Before Mr. Compton could reply, Felix Masters interposed. "John, my boy, that question is too simple for Compton. He is a regular warrior in the matter of logic. Of course, in this case, the inevitable conclusion would be that somebody, for reasons he alone knows best, had taken the trouble to have prepared and secreted large quantities of food and had arranged to appear to use very little of it. We have all heard of sleight-of-hand performances. I saw a fellow the other evening take dozens of eggs out of his hair, his whiskers, even his eyebrows! But I haven't the slightest idea that he really did so, have you?"

This time there was not only laughter but clapping of hands. John Brownlee turned and abruptly left the room.

"Poor John!" said his mother, restraining her laughter. "He's very nervous since his illness. A little matter excites him. His imagination has been stirred up by these absurd stories, until really he doesn't know what to think. I wish very much we could persuade him to go away for awhile, where he wouldn't hear any of these follies. I think when one has been through such an experience as his, one's nerves remain unstrung for a long time."

Mr. Masters promptly agreed with her and added that stories such as the public were now being fed did harm in many ways. The originator of them should by all means be taken in hand by the authorities and suppressed.

Miriam Brownlee's laugh was as silvery as it had been in days gone by. It floated out now and was followed by these words: "I can't understand why you gentlemen should be so solemn over it. Of course, some things are offensive to good taste. The gatherings in the street are horrid and shouldn't be permitted. But when they simply go off by themselves for an extraordinary picnic, what harm can it do? I haven't been so amused in a long time as I have been over the various accounts of this affair. Why can't we all take the fun that's in it and let it go?"

CHAPTER XVIII

AS THE HART
PANTETH
AFTER THE WATER
BROOKS

hether Miriam had planned that she would not look in the direction of David's eyes while this topic was up for discussion, he could not determine. He had certainly failed in every attempt to gain her attention, though he sat not far from her.

He had held himself to utter silence through it all, and no semblance of a smile was upon his face. The voice in which he at last broke his silence was startling in its sternness. "Do you all forget that you're speaking of the man who, only a very few days ago, met the members of this household on their way to the grave to bury their dead and, with a word, restored to them the light and joy of their

181

home?"

"Oh, Mr. Holman! Don't! DON'T!" cried Mrs. Brownlee, before retiring into her handkerchief to give vent to hysterical sobs.

It was then, for the first time, that Miriam darted a quick, annoyed glance at the astonished David as she made her hurried explanation. "Auntie's nerves were so fearfully disturbed during John's illness that she can't bear the slightest allusion to the subject. Auntie, dear, do try to control yourself. It's all over now, you know."

The sobs grew a little less violent. But the embarrassed guests looked at one another and didn't seem to know what to say next. This did not include David, who looked simply stern. He held himself as one who was keeping back further utterance by a strong effort. Mr. Masters came gracefully to the rescue.

"Holman is right. It isn't at all strange that John, under the circumstances, should be greatly excited and unable to control his sympathies. He's young yet and can't be expected to understand that his experience, unusual as it is, has its parallels even in modern history. Cases of suspended animation, even much longer than his, are upon record and are exceedingly well authenticated. Still, as I said, it isn't surprising that a young man whose mental condition had been exhausted by serious illness should have imbibed false ideas as to the causes of his recovery.

"The surprise is that mature people should allow themselves to become so confused that they imagine anything supernatural about it! I confess myself to have been disappointed about that. It's this tendency to credulity, which we find in certain persons we thought were better informed and bet-

ter balanced, that makes thoughtful men anxious
about the whole matter and unable to dismiss it as
something to be amused at for the moment. The
fact that the common people are agape over these
sleight-of-hand performances is to be expected and
smiled over. But when a few young and susceptible minds, like John's, for instance, may be seriously injured while we are laughing, it's a matter
for grave consideration. In my judgment we
should take hold of it with energy and, after decid-
ing what ought to be done, do it without further
delay.

"A crowd of unthinking, illiterate people is capable on very slight provocation of degenerating
into an unmanageable mob. They have secured a
leader this time who is very sharp and whose influence over them is becoming unlimited. In short,
I assure you, Miss Brownlee, that this whole subject, to thinking men who have the interests of the
country at stake, has its very serious side."

"Oh, yes," said Miriam, trying to throw off all
sense of anxiety and still speak lightly, "I suppose
you men must be serious sometimes. But we ladies, who can't do anything, should be allowed to
be amused. John, for instance, simply amuses me.
I'm not anxious about him, as his mother is. He's
merely a *boy*, carried away just now by strong personal feeling. But he is a Brownlee and has the
hard sense of generations to fall back upon. When
he recovers from this excitement — if the attack is
not made too much of — his common sense will
come to the rescue. I'm not afraid for John."

David Holman arose suddenly. His face was
very pale, and his eyes had a stern look with which
Miriam was not acquainted.

He made his adieus very briefly and got out

once more to the moonlit piazza. There he found John. The boy turned as he heard footsteps and, recognizing his friend, held out his hand. His voice trembled with excitement.

"Isn't it dreadful!" he said. "Simply horrible! The way they talk about that man! How am I to endure it? And *I* know what he did for me! Can't anyone be made to realize that I've been among the dead?"

David's only reply was to clasp the young fellow's hand with almost painful force. At last he said, "John, dear fellow! I sympathize with you utterly. Come and see me as soon as you can. We'll talk it all over. I can't talk tonight. I must get away."

What a ride he took over the familiar road once more in the solemn moonlight! What had he done? Others had laughed and sneered, some good-naturedly, some as cynics. But he had deliberately closed his eyes to probabilities and chosen for his companion for life one who ridiculed deeds that were to him divine! What had he been about, to imagine for a moment that he could influence to higher living one who had heard unmoved that voice of power? She had leaned over her cousin when he died. She had watched the light go out of his eyes and seen the clay grow beautiful in the majesty of death. Then, at the command of a voice that had power to reach the ears of death, she had seen him rise and go about in radiant health. Yet she could laugh and talk fluently and merrily about picnics and sleight-of-hand!

Was it only that morning, or was it ages ago, that he sat under the shadow of the rock and heard Philip Nelson tell the story of the breaking of bread for the hungry multitude? Every fiber of his being had responded to the power of the story. And she had ridiculed it and accepted the sneering explanation which set it down among the sleight-of-hand entertainments for the gaping crowd! *What had he done?* He who believed in this man as one sent from God! Sent perhaps — his tongue did not frame the words in his heart, but the hushed silence seemed to pulse with them — yet he had asked her, the storyteller of the evening, the one who had turned it all into ridicule, to be his wife!

Many times while lying on his couch of pain, David Holman had waded through deep waters, fought many battles, but never in his life had he felt the power of pain, awful soul pain, as he felt it that night.

He did not call upon Miriam Brownlee on the following evening. There was no good reason why he shouldn't, except that which he found in himself: In his bitter unrest of soul he shrank from meeting her just yet, shrank from the ordeal he felt might be before him. An overpowering desire to get away from everybody and be alone took possession of him. Tremendous questions begged to be settled. He had to define his position to Miriam. It by no means seemed the easy task he thought it to be only the day before. From his severe self-questioning he came out humiliated. It seemed that after waiting so many years he had at last been a creature of impulse. He admitted to his conscience that he had no clear story to tell Miriam. What was his position? He did not know. What he ought to have done was to have settled that first, instead of putting it aside as secondary, when in the depths of his soul he knew that it must forever be first with him.

Uncertain what step he should take next, he

waited in great and troubled doubt all day. The second morning's mail brought a letter that decided his immediate course. It was from Mr. Rothwell and contained an earnest invitation to him to spend the coming Festival Week in their city and make their house his home.

"I have learned," said the letter, "that our very dear friend, whom I believe you have special reason for being interested in, will be present during the week and will speak at some of the meetings. It occurred to me that this might be your opportunity to hear him and perhaps meet him personally, as I judged from some of your words when you were with us that you would like to do. We hope to have him as our guest at least part of the time."

Before David had finished this paragraph, he knew he had decided to attend the festival, though this had not been included in his previous plans.

"Mr. Rothwell!" said his father with evident interest when David made his invitation known. "That's an unusual honor, if all I hear of the Rothwells is true. You must have made a very favorable impression. Well, I would go by all means. I wish we could all attend. In my young days, nothing could keep me from being present during Festival Week."

The sentence closed with a sigh. After a moment he added regretfully, "It's a matter of grief to me that I haven't been able to give my family opportunities of this kind. I remember that the music of Festival Week used to linger with me through the year. What a treat it would be to Margaret! Ah, well, the future is before her and the rest of you. Perhaps, David, you can do for your sisters what I have not been able to. A friendship with the Rothwells is something to be desired. If there should be any opportunity to talk about business, there are some matters that I would like to have you bring up."

Evidently there was to be no difficulty in getting away for Festival Week; yet David was only half pleased. It was his nature to be frank, but he had said nothing about that paragraph in the letter which had decided him. Ought he to do so? He considered the question carefully and finally replied to it in the negative. He was not a mere boy, bound in honor to abide by his father's decisions. The very probability which pressed upon him that he should eventually have to decide against his father held him from making revelations before the time. The least cruel way was to be quite silent, until he knew just what he should say and just what he meant to do.

But to Frances the letter was shown. David, looking over her shoulder while she read, pointed silently to the important paragraph. Then they exchanged significant smiles that were tinged with sadness.

To Miriam, David wrote a very brief note to the effect that duty had called him away from home for a few days and that he would see her as soon as possible after his return. He paused over that word "duty." Was it *duty* that called? Undoubtedly it was inclination. Yes, he told himself, after careful study, it was also duty. He must know the ground on which he stood and understand his future so far as it could be known before he talked with Miriam Brownlee again. He owed that much to her; it was bewildering to him that he had not fully realized it before.

It was ten years since David Holman had been

inside the magnificent building where the services
of Festival Week were held. As a boy he had been
very familiar with the time-honored festival and
had looked forward eagerly to being present.

At that time the city was always in holiday attire
and was crowded to overflowing with visitors. He
had not been very deeply interested in the religious part of the service, but the music, he remembered, was entrancing. No doubt to his boyish
imagination everything was far more beautiful
than the reality would warrant. Still, the very
streets leading to the sanctuary, as he recalled
them, were festooned with evergreen and were
aglow with flowers and lights.

The music seemed to roll out with the continu-
ous strain: "O give thanks unto the Lord; for he is
good: because his mercy endureth forever." Many
times, lying on his bed of pain, he had closed his
eyes and seemed to hear again the jubilant outburst from the choir and the refrain by the people:
"Save now, I beseech thee, O Lord; O Lord, send
now prosperity."

As he made his way along the thronged streets
and neared once more the great building that had
delighted his beauty-loving heart as a boy, he
heard the same outburst of triumphant song: "O
give thanks unto the Lord; for he is good!"

David's heart thrilled with more than the old
feeling. He told himself that boyish imagination
had not exaggerated the scene. It was wonderful,
glorious! How many years it had been since he was
a member of that very choir! The memories of his
boyhood had at times seemed to be but dreams.
Some other boy, not he, had walked the streets and
seen the sights and heard the sounds about which
he lay and dreamed. It could never have been he!

But as he ran up the steps of the building on this
first evening of his arrival, he told himself that this
was real. He remembered it all. The words of the
choral, as they kept throbbing in the air, were real,
too — more real than in his happy, thoughtless
boyhood he had dreamed. "For his mercy endureth forever!"

Aye, it does! It has endured for me! echoed his
exultant heart.

"O magnify the Lord with me, and let us exalt
his name together. O Lord my God, I cried unto
thee, and thou hast healed me! Thou hast turned
for me my mourning into dancing: thou hast put
off my sackcloth, and girded me with gladness; to
the end that my glory may sing praise to thee, and
not be silent. O Lord my God, I will give thanks
unto thee for ever!"

Was the anthem written expressly for him?
Could words be made more fitted to his experiences? The music swelled and rolled through the
great building, and the young, exultant heart that
cried its eager "Amen!" to every refrain could
scarce contain its joy. How could he have thought
of staying away from the festival? This was his
place, the place of everyone who had a song of
gratitude to offer — and who had not? But none so
great as he. Surely he was blessed above all others
in this world! And his voice as well as his heart
took up the strain: "O give thanks unto the Lord;
for he is good."

The exalted mood did not last. The days passed,
and David, a regular attendant upon all the services, grew more accustomed to the sights and
sounds; he also became conscious of a painful reac-
tion. Between the services he mingled with the
people and heard much talk that was not in accord

with the exalted strains of music. Much of it seemed to him like meaningless repetition and some of it like solemn mockery. A great want for something better kept growing in his soul.

Dismayed and almost ashamed at this state of feeling, he kept his growing disappointment quite to himself and went back and forth with the Rothwells as one who shared their interest. By degrees it came to him that his disappointment, pain and eager desire for something better were shared by his friends. He could not have told just how he discovered this; they said no such words to each other. Possibly he heard it in Mary Rothwell's sigh as she walked down the aisle one evening, the service over for the day.

It had been a day of great enthusiasm, and the choral service of the evening had surpassed in grandeur any that had yet been given. But Mary Rothwell's face was serious even to sadness, and her sigh had expressed a kind of patient weariness.

Mr. Rothwell was being detained by some officials, and his sister, with David, waited for him near the door. Groups of people were standing about, conversing. Some of their talk arrested the attention of the two.

CHAPTER XIX

IF ANY MAN THIRST

 heard he was certainly coming," said one. "I was told by a man who I thought would be sure to know, and I have not missed a service in the hope of seeing him. But it's getting very late in the week."

"Do you think he will dare to come?" inquired a somber-faced man, drawing closer to the group. "I'm afraid he's in trouble. I heard from a very reliable source that there had actually been some sort of an attempt to arrest him — or, at least, a plan to do so, which was frustrated in an unexpected way. I think now that their scheme is to dispose of the whole matter quietly, without letting the people know anything about it. They're afraid of the crowd."

"They need to be!" exclaimed one in tones of subdued excitement. "The question is, Why are they afraid of him? Has anybody ever heard of his doing any harm? I'll tell you what I believe: He's a good man, and those who are trying to hurt him are no better than they should be."

"I believe more than that," came from another voice on the outskirts of the group, "and I've heard that he has hinted at something of the kind himself. What if he should prove to be the promised One?"

"What is that?" asked David Holman, suddenly pressing his way into the center of the company. "I beg your pardon, friends, but I overheard some of your words. Did I understand you to say that this stranger has made any claim such as you suggested?"

"Hush!" said a peremptory voice from the outside. "You need to be careful what you say. These are dangerous times. It's not safe to trust your tongue or your thoughts."

"You may trust me," said David earnestly. "I don't know very much about the man you're speaking of, but I'm deeply interested in him. I am sure of one thing: He cured me of a hopeless disease."

"Aye," said the voice who had made the startling claim. "A good many of us know that much. For my part, I don't see why we should need to know more, before we believe in him."

"You need to be careful, I tell you," cautioned the peremptory voice again. "It's dangerous business to proclaim oneself a friend of that man. Things are growing worse and worse, and before long they'll reach a climax. I know what I'm talking about, and I warn you as a friend. Don't gather in groups and talk about this matter. Above all, don't join with any of those who are known to be his friends. If you do, you'll certainly become objects of suspicion and very likely do him harm as well as yourselves."

Still David lingered in hope of hearing more, but the caution took effect at last. The people grew afraid of one another, and especially were they afraid of him, a stranger.

"Aren't you afraid of us?" asked Mary Rothwell with a gravely significant smile, as David at last moved back to her side. "We're his friends, remember, and we shall not hesitate to proclaim it from the housetop if we ever have opportunity."

"You heard the caution then?"

"Oh, yes, I heard. How little they understand him or his friends! As though personal safety could hinder us from acknowledging him everywhere, if he would only permit it."

David came late to the service next morning, although he had started out before any of the family. The strain of the past few days was telling on his nerves, and he had felt the need of getting away alone to quiet himself. He went for a long walk. As he entered the sanctuary the anthem was swelling through it in great waves of melody: "With joy shall ye draw water out of the wells of salvation." And then the continual refrain: "O give thanks unto the Lord; for he is good."

Following the burst of song came that peculiar hush a sensitive person can always feel when there is a great expectant audience. There was that this morning; the scene was strangely impressive. David, who had taken a seat that commanded a view of a large portion of the worshippers, was struck with the waiting attitude of the people. The very air throbbed with a sense of expectancy. The influence reached to the latecomer and commanded him. He felt as though another crisis in his life was approaching. From what source or how it came to be pressed upon him he could not divine. He did not understand his own heart, except that there seemed to be in it a great longing cry for God.

Suddenly penetrating the silence came a voice that he instantly recognized. No other voice had been to him what this one had.

The words spoken were clear, strong, commanding: "If any man thirst, let him come to me and drink."

David's heart beat so that it seemed to him it must be heard by those around him. He turned in the direction of the voice and looked.

Yet afterward, when he tried to tell Frances about it, he confessed that he could not describe the man nor explain the effect that his call had upon the great audience. He stood there calm and serious, nothing unusual in dress or manner. Simply a man among men. Yet what message was that, the echo of which still filled the air? "If any man thirst, let him come to ME and drink." The emphasis on the pronoun was marked and peculiar. The attention of everyone had been arrested, but it did not require close observation to discover that the audience was differently impressed. Unmistakable indignation, aye, absolute hatred, filled the faces of some. Others half arose, and the look in their eyes said they were ready to go to him at once, if that was what he meant.

The chorus rang out again, wonderful singing, swelling up among the arches and filling all the aisles like angelic presences. Perhaps it was the

best way to calm the multitude. Many heads were
bowed, but the thoughts of the worshippers were
not in the song. David, at least, could think of nothing but that commanding voice and those remarkable words. It had not been an invitation to come to
God or to prayer. It had been utterly unlike the
usual forms of speech. The pronoun had been in-
fused with personality.

It certainly was not surprising that the audience
hardly waited that morning for the formal dismiss-
al before their tongues were busy discussing the
strange interruption to the service. Among them
were some who said distinctly in low, awestricken
tones that this man, this remarkable stranger, must
be the promised One. Others quoted glibly from
the prophets and proved in their wisdom that this
man, who was the son of a carpenter and was himself a carpenter, could not possibly be the One for
whom the world was looking.

Meanwhile, the leaders of public affairs were
fairly ablaze with anger. Rumors of all sorts filled
the air. By night the story was afloat that officers
had been sent to the sanctuary itself to arrest the
bold stranger and had returned without him. They
affirmed that they had never heard any man speak
like him, and they had not felt it wise or safe to
arrest him.

Rumors of an excited debate in the council, hurriedly called together, were also rife. A sneering
voice had reportedly asked during this debate if
any of the leading people had taken part in the
popular excitement and had tried to prove that the
crowd — the rabble, the low and ignorant, who
were always agape over some new wonder — had
interested themselves in the stranger. Violent
measures were urged violently. But the story went

that certain clear-headed men of influence had been present who had urged that nothing rash be done.

The people were undoubtedly in a peculiar frame of mind, and it could not be denied that strange things had happened to make them feel as they did. Every step the leaders took had to be in exact accordance with the law. They were reminded that the stranger, even though it should prove that he was a deceiver and a traitor to his country, could nevertheless demand to be tried according to the law and must not be condemned until he was so tried.

It was said that these wise words were received angrily by certain leading men who did not hesitate to accuse the speaker of being himself interested in the deceiver and traitor. The outcome, they said, was simply the breaking up of the council in some confusion with nothing definite accomplished. How much of all this to believe, the anxious outsiders did not know. It was only too evident, however, that serious trouble lay ahead. By degrees the great crowds of people on the streets scattered to their various homes, and the city grew outwardly as quiet as usual; but in reality it seethed and boiled with excitement.

It is very difficult to describe such excitement as was felt by some of them — for instance, David Holman. Every nerve in his body quivered with an emotion that was akin to pain. He had heard once again the voice that had made it endurable for him to live, and it had thrilled him as even that first message had not done. It had been with the utmost difficulty that he had held himself from outward demonstration of any sort. When that strong, solemn voice filled the sanctuary with the call, "If any

man thirst, let him come to me and drink," every
fibre of David Holman's being longed to cry out, "I
thirst, and I come!" He would have been willing
then and there to bow at the feet of the stranger
and ask his way. Willing! He longed to do it. Only
the fear that he should in this way have jeopard-
ized that stranger's interests held him back.

He walked home with Mary Rothwell in almost
utter silence, a long walk away from the turmoil of
the crowded city. For a time they kept utter silence.
David felt that he had no words for the occasion,
and his companion did not seem anxious to break
the spell of silence. He felt, however, that she was
by no means so disturbed as he was. The desire to
know what she thought of all the strange events of
the day forced him at last to speech.

He began as one who had no need for explanation. She would know what he meant.

"What are we to think?"

Perhaps her reply was the crowning surprise of
that day. "I long ago settled that question for myself, my friend. I know exactly what I think."

He turned eager, hungry eyes upon her. If she
did, she ought to be able to help him.

"Won't you tell me then?" he said, as one who
grasped at possible relief. "My soul is in such a
tumult as I never before realized was possible. If
someone who has passed over the road before is at
rest — and your voice sounds as though you are —
then surely the way can be pointed out to another."

"Yes, if you're ready for it. My rest is to believe
every word that my Friend says — *every word* —
and follow his directions as closely as I can and,
where I don't understand, trust. A great deal of it I
don't understand. I can feel, Mr. Holman, that you

want to ply me with questions, and I tell you frankly that I cannot answer them. I don't know enough — not yet. I know only this: that he comes from God and that as fast as he leads I will follow. He makes no mistakes."

"Miss Rothwell, I beg you to speak plainly. I'm not questioning you from idle curiosity. It's a matter of life or death to me. Do you mean that you trust this man as your Savior?"

The tremendous thought was put at last into actual words, and he held his breath waiting for her answer.

Mary Rothwell could feel the blood rolling in waves over her face, but her voice was steady and sweet. "He has saved *me*, Mr. Holman. He has come entirely contrary to all my preconceived ideas. He lives contrary to them every day. He shocks my prejudices in numberless ways. But when I study his acts carefully, I don't find that he shocks my knowledge, only my preconceived notions, my prejudices. I don't know why he came as he did nor why he lives in poverty and obscurity, even in humiliation. But when I study my Scriptures I can't help but discover what I never saw before — that he was promised so to come. I don't know how long these conditions are to last. But if they lasted forever, I would still trust him implicitly and know that what he did was always best. Am I being plain enough?"

David drew a long, quivering sigh as he replied in a voice that trembled with emotion: "If you feel all that, you may indeed be at rest. I would that I could arrive at such a stopping place, but my brain whirls when I try to follow you."

"I'll tell you what you need, Mr. Holman." The quality of Mary's voice had changed. Her words carried conviction with them. "You need to see this Teacher, to talk with him and be helped by him, as no other can help. If he comes to us for rest before he leaves the city, I mean to try to arrange so that you can have a private interview with him. I'm sure it's what you need. No words of mine can explain or describe the power he has over human hearts. But now that you've heard him speak again, I think you must have an idea of what I mean."

"Yes," he said, his breath escaping him again. "Yes, I understand in part. What it would be to me to see and talk with him alone — I can't put into words."

The tense strain upon his emotions lingered through the night and followed him into the quiet of the Sabbath morning. His host and family went early to attend their several classes. He accompanied Mr. Rothwell to the door and then, promising to join the family later for the service, moved on down the street. His brain was still in such a tumult that the quiet and inactivity in the sanctuary seemed unendurable, and he resolved to try to walk off some of his excitement.

He strode slowly, however, down the quiet street. The day did not invite haste. The usual sights and sounds of the city streets were absent. A Sabbath calm seemed to rest upon the world. The very air was still and balmy. The flutter of wings was in all the trees as the birds chirped sweetly about their own affairs. David, usually so susceptible to nature's influences, felt a strange sense of irritation at the calm which surrounded him. How could earth and air and sky be so entirely at rest, or even the senseless birds chirp so contentedly about their nests and their housekeeping, when such colossal interests were knocking at human hearts?

Just a little ahead of him, groping his way along in the uncertain manner belonging to the blind, was a man close to his own age. David felt his heart swell with pity at the sight. He might be almost irritated over the beauty of the morning, but it would be a dreadful thing not to be able to see this lovely earth.

He readily overtook the hesitating steps and asked sympathetically, "How long have you been blind, my friend?"

The man turned his sightless eyes in the direction of the sound and answered with that melancholy cadence in his voice which the hopelessly blind seem to have: "I never knew, sir, what it was to see."

The answer struck David Holman's heart like a blow. Always blind! And he, who had been laid on a bed of pain for a few years, had felt often that his burden was greater than he could bear. Yet he could always see his friends and in intervals of pain watch the sunsets and the ever-changing clouds. What would have become of him had he lost the use of his eyes? Yet this man lived always in perpetual darkness! He lingered with him, accommodating his pace to the other's halting steps and expressing words of sympathy. The thought that was now never far from his mind came this time in the form of curiosity as to what would happen if this man and the wondrous stranger should ever meet. It caused him to ask next if the man had any hope of ever being able to see.

"Well," said the blind man hesitatingly, "I can't exactly say that I have any hope of it. I was born blind, you see — but some things have made me say, 'What if?' But I don't get any further than that."

He was evidently afraid to speak more plainly. David's heart met him halfway. "I understand you," he said quickly. "You needn't be afraid of such words with me. I know wonderful cures have been wrought. Who should know, if not I? Have you ever met the man we're both thinking of?"

"Oh, no! If only I could — just once! Who knows what might — "

Then he stopped, as one who dared not say more.

CHAPTER XX

TO OPEN
THE BLIND EYES

ust then they turned the corner. They had taken only a few steps on this new street before David became aware of footsteps behind them and the murmur of voices. He glanced back, and for the moment it seemed to him as though his very heart stood still.

Behold, coming with quickened footsteps almost at their side was the stranger. Philip Nelson walked beside him, talking earnestly. Following them were the other men who attached themselves to him, and following them still was a small company of boys and street loungers. It was as Miriam Brownlee had said. "The rabble were always following close at his heels."

202

Without taking time for consideration, David laid his hand on the arm of his blind companion and spoke quickly. "My friend, the opportunity of a lifetime is at hand. The man we've been thinking of is just behind you. He and his followers are coming down this street."

He distinctly felt the tremor which ran through the man's frame, but no word was spoken. The man merely stopped and stood perfectly still. David, who had taken his arm the better to direct his steps, stopped also.

At that moment the company just behind moved alongside them, and the eyes of the strange physician were immediately fastened on those blind ones.

Instinctively David dropped back a pace or two, for the man was speaking to his companion in low tones. Then he bent down and gathered some of the clay at his feet. With a few touches of it he made a kind of paste, which he spread over the blind eyes. Then came the bewildering direction, quite as if this were an ordinary occurrence. "Go to the fountain over there and wash your eyes."

Immediately, at a signal from him, the company moved on, and David and his companion were left behind. For the moment David forgot him.

He looked after that advancing form with inexpressible longing in his heart. Oh, to have Philip Nelson's opportunity for a single half hour! Oh, to be able to ask a single one of the questions that were surging through his mind! Of course, he must not intrude. These friends had been chosen from among the crowd and especially and personally invited to keep their teacher company. It would be unpardonable to join them uninvited.

Then he turned and looked at those mud-plastered eyes. It was well that the man could not know what an object had been made of him! Why had it been done?

"What are you going to do next?" David asked.

The intensity of the reply was impressive. "I am going over to that fountain. I would go to the world's end and attempt the impossible at that man's direction."

"Yes," said David, "so would I. Come with me. I'll take you there."

The streets were by no means as quiet as they had been. People were beginning to pass in groups on their way to the early service. They all bestowed curious glances on David's companion and had a second curious glance for David himself. Some of the words floated back to them.

"Those are peculiar-looking people! What do you suppose that older one has on his eyes?"

"Dear me! Isn't that blind Joe? Who has disfigured him? Or perhaps it's some new medicine he's trying!" The boys, those omnipresent creatures, especially upon city streets, began to gather from only they knew where and follow the two, shouting funny speeches after Joe and laughing derisively over his strange appearance.

It was a walk for David Holman to remember. Never but once before had he been the subject of ridicule on the street. The remembrance of it caused his face to burn. He had been overcome with liquor so that he staggered. The quick-witted boys had discovered it and followed after him, imitating his faltering steps. The contrast was striking, but it was not pleasant to be ridiculed for any cause. He had no intention of leaving his blind friend to grope his way alone, but unconsciously he quickened his steps. He would be glad when the ordeal was over.

At last they reached the fountain. The blind man, bending toward the sound of its splashing waters, washed away the mud from his eyes and in doing so washed away forever the veil that had hidden the world from his sight.

Who shall undertake to put into words a description of that man's sensations when his eyes first saw those brilliant flashes of color in tree and flower and wing of bird? He trembled and staggered and would have fallen but for David's arm suddenly thrown about him.

"What is it?" asked David, his excitement almost equal to the other's. "Lean on me. What's the matter?"

"I can see!" said the man. He didn't shout the words. Instead, they were almost a whisper, exultant, yet awestricken. "Oh, God! I tell you I can see! Where is that man? Where did he go? Take me to him! I could fall down and worship him."

If they had attracted attention as they walked toward the fountain, what shall be said of the sensation they made as they hurried back through the town? It happened that blind Joe was a well-known character. People were accustomed to seeing him grope his way through unfamiliar streets, putting out his hands carefully on either side to feel if the way was clear. Here he was, with head erect, taking long strides over the road, avoiding the crowds on the walks as only one could do who had full use of his eyes. Tongues were busy on every side.

"Why, that isn't blind Joe!"

"Yes, it is! Don't you suppose I know Joe?"

"But that man can see, I tell you, as well as I can."

"It looks as if he can — and Joe was born blind! There is some mystery about it. I wonder who that other fellow is? I never saw him before."

Still other groups stared and commented.

"Why, of course, that's Joe Andrews! Haven't I lived next door to the family for twenty years? I don't pretend to understand it, but I know that's he."

Then Joe, his way blocked by the gathering crowd, stopped, smiling.

"You're right," he said cheerily. "I'm Joe Andrews, sure enough. I don't wonder that you're astonished. You can't be more so than I am. Let me tell you about it."

Significant glances were exchanged among the groups of people as they listened to the simple yet astounding facts. Many of them knew, even before a description of him was reached, that the wonder-working stranger and the man who had roused the excitement of the people and the hatred of the rulers were the same. The people were interested, but troubled. At last one spoke: "What we should do is report this case to the authorities. These are anxious times, and for us to be here talking with a man who has been cured of blindness, without taking steps to have the matter looked into, would make our lives worth very little."

This called forth an eager discussion. Some did not hesitate to affirm that there had evidently been a wonderful cure performed. They thought the authorities ought to be glad, instead of making a fuss about it. But, for the most part, the people were afraid. Before he fully realized what was taking place, David found himself in the midst of what might almost have been called an impromptu trial. As they moved on down the street, which was every moment thronged with more people, it became apparent that certain men who stood high in official circles had joined them and were closely questioning Joe Andrews. Joe had only his simple story to tell, but it was surprising what sneers and insinuations greeted it.

"I have no idea that he was born blind," said one of the wise men. "You can't trust these fellows when they want to expand a story. He's been partially blind for some time. I've seen him groping his way about town. Probably he was never so badly off as he imagined. These cases sometimes recover sight very suddenly. There's nothing to get excited about."

"There's his mother!" exclaimed a boy on the outskirts of the crowd. "She'll know whether he was blind or not."

Somebody immediately stopped the father and mother, who were trying to weave through the crowds, not toward but away from their son. They were not only excited but frightened. They realized more fully than did some the danger of having to do with the strange doctor. The poor mother shook her head in answer to some of the questions, but she could not bring herself to deny her son's identity.

"Oh, yes, he's our boy. Of course, I would know Joe anywhere. Yes, sir, he was born blind. Oh, I don't know how he was cured! How should I? We have but this minute heard of it. Why don't you ask Joe? He's the only one who can tell about it."

This, of course, had already been done but had not proved satisfactory. It would have seemed that only one conclusion could be reached by the facts, yet these wise men reached another.

"Very well," they said at last, addressing Joe.

"You have occasion to thank God for having restored your full sight. It will be well for you to discover what He means by such an act of mercy. As for the fellow to whom you credit the cure, remember that the less you say about him the better for you. We know too much of him already. He is a dangerous fellow."

Joe's newly recovered eyes flashed. He had been blind but not stupid. He smiled triumphantly in the face of the man who had cautioned him and spoke out boldly.

"That's very extraordinary. A 'dangerous fellow,' and yet he has cured me of blindness. Since the world began, no one has known of a man born blind being cured. You say God cured me. I haven't a doubt of it. But he certainly did it through that man. Now we both believe that God does not hear the prayers of dangerous fellows! How is it all to be explained?"

Then the dignified public officials forgot their dignity and stooped to sneers and taunts. They reminded Joe Andrews of his humble birth, his lack of education, the inability of his parents to instruct him. Indeed, they ran all over the humilities and privations of his life, impressing upon him the folly of his presuming to instruct such ones as they were! If he were to be thus injured by God's gift of sight, it would have been better for him to have remained blind. Through it all, Joe kept his temper with an ease that David Holman could have envied.

It was very true, he replied calmly, that he did not know much. He had had few opportunities for knowledge. But two things he knew: He had been blind all his life until about an hour ago, and now he could see distinctly. Yes, he knew a third thing.

He knew the man who had given him sight, and he meant to find him and thank him, even if it took the rest of his life to do so.

And then David, feeling that the restored man needed no more help from him, escaped from the crowd and made his way by a side street to the sanctuary. Evidently the streets were not the place for one who was trying to steady his pulses and think dispassionately.

As he left the service that evening, just as he reached the sidewalk, someone touched his arm. He turned quickly to meet the earnest eyes of his companion of the morning.

"I wanted to see you again," he began eagerly, "to thank you for your great help this morning. But for you I might not have understood...well, sir, you know.... More than that, I want to tell you the rest of the story. You said this morning that you believed in that man. I don't know how much you meant, perhaps no more than I did then. But I mean more now. I have seen him."

"Do you mean since this morning?"

"I didn't see him this morning," said the man with a sudden smile of joy radiating his face. "But tonight, just at sunset — I saw the sunset! Can you imagine what a sight that was to me? Then I saw *him* and knew him in an instant. No, please, don't ask me how. I can't tell. He is unlike any other.

"I'm to be excommunicated from the congregation — you guessed as much this morning, didn't you? What question do you think he asked me tonight? The first words he spoke to me were, 'Do you believe on the Son of God?' I wish I could describe to you the feeling that that question gave me — a strange sensation all through me. At first I couldn't speak. Then I said, almost in a whisper,

'Who is he, that I may believe on him?' Will you bend your head a little, sir, so that I may tell you the exact words of his reply? 'I who speak to you am He!' Yes, sir, those were the words! I can never forget them. They are true, TRUE! I know it! I am sure of it!"

David Holman walked the streets that evening as one who saw not. He did not realize where he walked; nor did he care. His one desire was to get away from people and let his brain take in and dwell upon those solemnly significant words: "I who speak to you am He!"

After that, said his heart to him, what need you any further witness?

He tramped about over the hills that skirted the town until his body at least was tired. Then, realizing that the hour was growing late and that his host might be troubled as to what was detaining him, he hastened to the Rothwells' home.

At the door stood Mary, and he remembered afterward the look of solemn joy on her face as she greeted him. "Mr. Holman? I'm so glad you have come! I've been watching for you. Our friend is here, and he will see you in his room. You may go up at once if you wish — you know the room? The one you occupied the first night you spent with us."

David held out his hand to the girl, his voice tremulous with emotion: "God bless you for getting me this opportunity. I shall never forget it."

Then he turned and ran up the stairs two steps at a time, his heart beating in great thuds, his face pale with expectation. Tapping gently at the door, he received an instant invitation to enter. He turned the knob and was at last alone in the presence of the One whose power over him was henceforth to be absolute and eternal.

They were walking to town together on the following afternoon — Mary Rothwell and David Holman. He had been talking so earnestly that he did not realize the distance they had come nor the fact that they were in one of the crowded thoroughfares of the city. He had been telling, as nearly as such an experience could be put into words, about his interview of the night before.

Certain moments of that interview he never expected to try to describe to any human being. But there was much that could be given to a sympathetic listener, especially to one who understood the matter better than he did himself. In truth, he questioned her as to the possible meaning of this or that word which the Master had spoken to him.

She had smiled significantly when he first used that phrase, and he had gone back to the sentence and said reverently, "My Master." Then Mary Rothwell had felt that the interview had accomplished its object, and this troubled soul was at rest.

Suddenly David was recalled to the immediate present in a startling way.

CHAPTER XXI

I WILL DECLARE
THY NAME
UNTO MY BRETHREN

s they began to feel the necessity of picking their way through the crowded streets, David became aware, in the manner that no one understands but has experienced, that a pair of eyes from out of the throng was following him. He turned his head in the direction of a carriage that was just then blockaded, met the owner of that intense pair of eyes and lifted his hat to Miriam Brownlee. The bow was returned by a bend of the head so slight that he was almost in doubt as to whether she had bowed at all. Then her carriage moved on.

In vain David tried to continue the train of thought thus interrupted. The vision of Miriam

Brownlee was like a breath from another world,
blown suddenly across his brain. She was at home
then. He hadn't thought of it. Indeed, as he reflected he realized that he had not so much as remembered that he was in the city where she lived.
His association with her had been almost exclu-
sively connected with her aunt's home. Years ago
he had called upon her at her father's house. But it
was before he had realized any deep interest in her,
and the call had made no distinct impression.

The questions that arose now were, How long
had Miriam been in town, and what had occa-
sioned her return?

He had been under the impression that she had
expected to spend the season with her aunt. But as
he recalled the past, he became aware that this was
only an impression and that he had no distinct
knowledge concerning her. If she had been at
home a long time she must have thought it very
strange that he hadn't called on her. Indeed, as he
considered it, he admitted that it was surprising
that he had not interested himself to call upon her
mother. As matters now stood between him and
Miriam, this would have been obviously proper,
but the simple truth was that he had been so absorbed in a subject of infinitely more importance
that he had forgotten calls altogether.

Did this account for Miriam's haughty stare? No
other word would describe the look upon her face.
An angry stare — and she had made no attempt to
hold the carriage long enough for him to get to her.

I'm afraid I've been rude, was his mental decision. She is, perhaps, justified in feeling hurt.

Evening found him at the Brownlee homestead.
Miss Miriam was at home and entertaining callers
— among them Mr. Compton, whom David did

not remember pleasantly. There was nothing for him but to take a seat among the guests and try to be one of them. Within his heart was a sense of incongruity. He found it well-nigh impossible to join in the lively conversation which his entrance had interrupted for the moment but which flowed on easily again.

The topic under discussion was an entertainment given recently. All present save him had apparently been at the entertainment, and they were comparing notes. Criticism was unsparing; some of the performers were unmercifully ridiculed. It did not seem to David that the audience, if this were a specimen, could really have been entertained. It all represented another world from his. And those people, he reflected, at least four of them, are connected with the congregation, and this has been its great anniversary week. They seem not to have known of it!

He had chosen a seat as close to Miriam as he could, and at the first opportunity addressed her. "I was very much surprised to see you this afternoon. I had no idea you were in town."

"Indeed! Didn't you know I lived in this city?" The question was asked laughingly, but the tone had a sting in it for David's ear.

He tried to explain with some confusion that he had had the impression she was still with her aunt.

"Oh, I come home quite frequently," she said brightly. "But I don't think my departure for this city was any more sudden than your own."

Clearly they were not making any advance under cover of this surface talk. Watching his opportunity, he asked in an undertone if it wouldn't be possible to see her alone for a few minutes. He was answered quite coldly that it was quite out of the question; the callers were her guests, of course, and must be entertained.

Immediately she returned to the conventional tone. "Are you having a pleasant visit in town, Mr. Holman? I noticed this afternoon that you were so much engaged that I hardly dared intrude, even with a bow."

The low, silvery laugh that accompanied these words he had been accustomed to calling sweet. He wondered how he ever could have!

"I've had a wonderful week," he said with seriousness. "A week to be remembered forever. Certain experiences connected with it I'm eager to tell you. I must return home tomorrow. A note from my father, which I received this evening, hurries me. I'd hoped to see you at your aunt's as soon as I returned. Don't you return there soon?"

This much he accomplished for her ear alone, but her answer grated. "I'm not planning to. As I mentioned, I live at home. It must be hard for both you and your friends to have your visit cut short. Is Miss Rothwell as much of a rosebud as I intimated? If so, your tastes must have changed, for you certainly appeared to be enjoying the variety when I saw you this afternoon."

He looked at her bewildered. The question flashed through his mind whether she could possibly be jealous of Mary Rothwell. He discarded it at once as a thought unworthy of him and of her. But there appeared before him, then and there without any volition on his part, a vision of the fair young woman with whom he had spent the afternoon and of their talk together. The sharp contrast between the two gave him a strange sense of pain. In the midst of these thoughts, he was replying with dignity to Miriam. "Miss Rothwell has been very kind to me, and I have reason for gratitude for the courtesies received. I have, however, seen very little of her and, to be quite frank, have been so absorbed with other thoughts as to leave little room for any person except one."

Miriam reflected on the identity of the one exception and misled herself. Even David Holman, unconventional as he was, could hardly speak to her in that tone and mean anything other than a personal compliment.

A pretty flush softened the haughty lines of her face for a moment, and her tones were gentler. "I hope the absorption proved agreeable? Mama has been surprised at not receiving a call from you earlier. But I reminded her that Festival Week was crowded with meetings and that very proper religious people did not consider social calls in order — though no one would have imagined that you would be so conventional with us."

It was not conventionality, he told her earnestly; it was absorption. Then, dropping his voice still lower, he pleaded for an opportunity for just a few words with her in private. He had revelations to make. There had come to him not so much a change of purpose as of vision. He had been blind and had received sight. Wouldn't it be possible to excuse herself to her guests for a few minutes and go out with him? Couldn't they do some errand or accomplish some end that would make it appear reasonable?

Miriam was sure that nothing of the kind was feasible. Mama would be shocked at such a breach of etiquette. At least one of the guests was a stranger to her mother and sister. "Besides," she added, "to be entirely frank, I don't think it would be well for us to have a visit together tonight. You are in one of your exalted moods. People who have been in contact with Mary Rothwell always are. I'd be certain to shock you. I prefer to wait until you return to the level of everyday life."

After that David shortened his call. He felt dazed and troubled and was in a hurry to get away. Miriam accompanied him to the front hall, but it was nearly as public as the parlor. He murmured something to her about writing as soon as he reached home, without knowing what reply she gave, and at last was outside in the quiet night. He took off his hat and passed his hand wearily over his forehead as he walked. His brain seemed to need cooling.

The stars were far away and barely visible. Wouldn't it be good to get away from all the bewilderments of earth, up there? What had occurred to make life stretch itself before him as such a complex thing? Very little had passed between him and Miriam, certainly, but that little had power to sting. He had looked forward to telling her the experience of the night before, as he could tell it to no other. But she hadn't cared to hear it. Now he wasn't sure that he could ever tell her.

He sat up late trying to plan his life. It was linked with another life whose happiness must ever be his first consideration. But there was more than that. It was linked for time and for eternity with a divine life which his duty and his privilege would be to serve. Would Miriam Brownlee ever be in accord with the convictions which he knew must now govern him? And if she were not? Why, then he must walk that road alone. Only one thought stood out boldly. The pledge he had taken in that other room that night was to be held sacred and supreme. Not mother nor father nor Miriam

Brownlee herself was ever to come between his soul and that.

Full of other interests as the week had been, there had yet been time for business matters. David Holman had reason to believe that his father would be gratified with the result.

He was more than gratified and spoke more frankly than was his habit. He had not imagined that such an arrangement could be brought about. David had shown himself a businessman of marked ability. Why wouldn't he give up his ideas of a profession and go into business with his father? These new openings he had himself arranged would afford a splendid opportunity. Couldn't they decide to join their interests and work together?

David saw an eager, hopeful light in his mother's face. She would like such an arrangement because it would anchor her son at home. He was sorry the proposition had been offered just then. It forced him to speak before he had determined what to say.

Curiously enough it was Margaret who helped him to a little more time by opposing the idea almost petulantly. For her part she did not want David, with his education that fitted him for taking his place in the world, to settle down to be a mere fruit-raiser.

Her father showed promptly that he was hurt by her words. He replied coldly that "mere fruit-raising" had furnished a very good support for the family for years. Without it David would hardly have received the education in which she took so much pride. But of course David was not to be compelled to enter into partnership with his father. It was a mere proposition, which he was to treat as he thought best.

Evidently the time had come for David to speak. He made it very clear that he had no such feeling for the business as Margaret had expressed. He said frankly that to work in the open air among the vines was a delight to him; he sometimes felt closer to God's handiwork there than anywhere else. Nevertheless, he was not ready for any partnership nor for positive decisions of any sort regarding his life's work.

If his father was willing to have him continue for the present, working under his direction and attending to any outside business that he chose to place in his hands, it would be the arrangement that he would like the best. He might be glad in the near future to discuss the question of partnership. But he was too unsettled about his plans at present to discuss them intelligently.

This reply by no means satisfied his father. Mr. Holman had not hesitated to say within his family that David was losing a great deal of time, and he did not understand why. Having lost so many years, it was important for him to settle quickly what he intended to do and to set about it at once. This idea he now put into plain language for David's ear and asked what was holding him from a decision.

Thus pressed, there was nothing for David but frankness. He took one or two thoughtful walks down the room while his father waited, regarding him curiously. Frances, with her head bent over her work, knew that her telltale face must be crimson.

"What I have to say, sir," began David at last, "will, I fear, cause you pain. That is what makes me hesitate. Yet perhaps the time has come when I should speak. My uncertainty with regard to my future grows out of the fact that I recognize a new Master. I've come into personal contact again with the man you have already heard so much about and have reached certain astounding conclusions concerning him. I meant to talk this whole matter over with you quietly, Father, and not startle you by the suddenness of my revelations. But perhaps it's as well this way. No amount of talk can prepare one for such words. The simple truth is, sir, that I believe we have in the person of that man the promised Savior we have been looking for these many years."

At this the mother gave a little frightened cry: "Oh, my son! Don't!"

Frances dropped her work and sat with her eyes fixed on her brother, with a face from which apparently every drop of blood had receded.

Margaret sewed steadily on with the slightest possible shadow of a smile or else a sneer playing about her mouth.

As for Mr. Holman, he had been a man of few words all his life, and generally he had his emotions well under control. At that moment his squarely cut chin seemed squarer than usual; his lips were set in a firm, thin line; and his restless eyes seemed to burn. Yet his voice was low and wonderfully controlled when at last he spoke: "You do well to speak plainly, David, though you use such awful words. I like to understand what I'm to expect. If I am to be struck to the heart by my own son, it is well to know it.

"I've brought up a boy, it seems, who cares no more for the parents and sisters who have sacrificed and suffered for his sake than to yield himself to the control of the first imposter who tramps over the country followed by a rabble. It is humiliating to the last degree, but I can bear it. I've had hard blows before. I ought to be used to suffering, especially where you are concerned.

"But I can speak plainly, too. We will understand one another. So long as you, sir, hold yourself away from any outward association with this accursed imposition, and keep your wild fancies entirely to yourself, I am willing to try to think that they are vagaries of a diseased brain that will pass away. But just so surely as you join the ignorant crowd in following that imposter about; mention to others the insane idea you have just now advanced; or have anything whatever to do with him or his friends in any way, from that hour you are no son of mine. And no house of mine shall shelter you, and no children of mine shall have anything to do with you — so help me God! I advise you to be very careful in making your final decisions. When I make mine, you know very well that I mean them."

Mrs. Holman's voice interrupted again. "Oh, Father, don't say that! Don't! DON'T!"

"I have said it." The father's voice had never been firmer. "You all know me — what I say I mean. If David wants to belong to us and to have us do for him the very best we can in the future what we have done during his long years of helplessness, so be it. He is welcome. He is to make his own choice. But an apostate and a blasphemer I cannot and will not harbor in my house. Our name has never yet been tarnished by disloyalty to country or to God. If it must be now, I will do what I can to show the world and the congregation that it is through no sin of mine."

CHAPTER XXII

GIVE US HELP
FROM TROUBLE

The days that followed were among the hardest that the Holman family had ever borne, though each member of it tried to act as though nothing very serious had happened. The conversation, or rather, the father's speech, had been cut short by the arrival of a man to see him on business. He did not revert to the subject again until that evening just before family worship.

Then he said that, painful as it was for him to refer to the scene of the morning, there was one other word that he ought to have spoken. He had learned only very recently what utter shipwreck Philip Nelson had made of himself, giving up his business and his home and following a tramp about the country! It seemed incredible, yet he had taken pains to inform himself of the truth of the report. It only helped to prove how dangerous a thing it was to have to do with falsehoods of this nature. He trusted that after what he had said, no more would be necessary. Yet he felt it his duty to add that hereafter his house would be closed to Philip Nelson, and his family was to understand that he was to be treated, should they chance to meet, as a stranger.

Whether he understood fully the blow that he was thus administering to his eldest daughter may be doubted. Because he was always a reserved man with his family, it had been difficult for his daughters to confide in him. Frances especially had been timid and reserved in his presence. It comforted her now to think he might not understand what Philip Nelson's friendship was to her.

Margaret tried to be sympathetic. "I'm awfully sorry for you, Frances, but I'm awfully vexed with Philip. It does seem to me that he might have thought of you before letting his insane folly go to such lengths. It is really very surprising. Philip never seemed like that sort of man."

Frances, who had resolved upon silence, was tempted to speech. "I don't quite understand what sort of man you mean. You see how David feels about this matter."

"Oh, I'm not surprised at David. His nervous system has been weakened by illness, and he is in a state to be easily imposed upon temporarily. He'll come out of it all right. If family ties are not strong enough to hold him, Miriam Brownlee will be able to manage it. I have no fears for David. He has never tramped the country with the rabble, and I don't believe he ever will."

Her sister was regarding her steadily. Should she speak again or be silent? She resolved upon speech. "Those are not your own ideas, Margaret. None of the words you have spoken tonight are like you. I think you're sorry for me. But, believe me, you can't express that sorrow in the platitudes of Felix Masters. I would rather have one word from you than a volume from him. I'm not afraid for David, either, nor for Philip. Both of them will do what is right, and I would have neither of them do other than that. There are interests far stronger than human friendships."

"Upon my word," said Margaret, "I believe you are one of them yourself!"

She was not asked to explain what she meant, and it was not mentioned between them again.

David, because he could not decide what he ought to say, was also silent. He went in and out from the home as usual. He interested himself deeply and satisfactorily in his father's business, going over details with him and answering business letters so that the father longed for the proposed partnership. Moreover, he believed that such would be David's decision. A keen-brained young man, as he evidently was, could not lightly throw away such an opportunity. The father firmly believed that, having been firm himself, he needed only to bide his time and all would be well. David was not like that visionary, ill-balanced young man Philip. So he advised with his son on business matters and deferred to his judgment in a way that would have been flattering had he spoken to a mind less preoccupied with grave interests.

David certainly had much to think about. Settled in regard to the matter of supreme moment, he was yet no nearer a decision as to his next step than before. He had written a note to Miriam, pledging himself to return very soon to her city and assuring her he would have important news to communicate to her when he came. The half-formed resolve to write what he had to say to her passed away.

By some strange freak of the heart he invariably succeeded, when away from Miriam, in believing that all she needed to bring her into accord with the new life he meant to live was a careful explanation of the entire subject. He assured himself this could be done much better by word of mouth than on paper, so he waited with what patience he could. He was unwilling to leave his father just then with business cares resting heavily upon him. Moreover, wouldn't it be better for him to know positively just what his next step would be before seeing Miriam?

As the days passed, and he still did not see his way clear to leaving home, he wrote long letters to Miriam on almost every subject but the one that engrossed his thoughts. Then came a letter from a distant part of the state, demanding personal attention. The father elected David to go. He welcomed the duty. To get away from everybody he knew and think out his problem alone was perhaps what he needed.

The first person he met after settling himself in a hotel was Philip Nelson.

"Are you truly here?" he exclaimed, stopping short in the street.

"I might respond in the same manner," said Philip, smiling. "You're the last person I expected to meet. What does it mean?"

David turned at once in the direction his friend had been going. After explaining his own errand briefly, he asked with an eagerness that could not be suppressed, "And now for your story. Are there any new developments?"

"That depends. I don't know how well you've kept posted since I last saw you. Do you know that we are all in this part of the world and that we had to get away from the town where we last met?"

"Is *he* here, Philip? You 'had to get away'? Why?"

"His life was in danger. When it was discovered that Joe Andrews had been made to see, the feeling against his Deliverer became intense. It culminated in a deliberate effort to take him away! Their failure can be accounted for only on the ground that he did not choose to allow it. It is well known that the country is in the hands of a few, and those few are his enemies. Still I think they feared the people. It was hardly reasonable to suppose the crowds who were receiving daily benefits at his hands could turn against him at once — though I don't think the crowd can be depended upon. It thinks one thing today and another tomorrow. Doesn't it seem incredible that such a man should be hunted from place to place like an outlaw?"

David's gesture was almost one of impatience. "I don't know what to think," he said. "Look where your own logic leads you. If this man were what you believe him to be, how could any people, however high in power, withstand him?"

"David," asked his friend significantly, "do you mean to say 'if'? I thought you had reached the point where you dropped all 'ifs' and said, 'I know.' "

David's sensitive face flushed. But he answered the rebuke with a smile as he said: "Perhaps that is well deserved. In my heart there are no 'ifs,' but I don't understand."

"Nor do I. May I answer your question by a quotation? 'He is brought as a lamb to the slaughter, and as a sheep before her shearers is dumb, so he openeth not his mouth.' Do you remember those words and their connection? What do they mean? It's all a mystery. He understands perfectly that there's a conspiracy against him. He even knows more about it than we do, and he more than hints that his enemies will be successful. And yet he says — has, in fact, said it more than once to different classes of people — that he is the Son of God, the promised Savior of the world! I heard him in a public meeting read those very words from which I've quoted and apply them to himself! The people were so angry that they tried to take his life, and they do not understand why he escaped them."

They extended their walk well into the evening. Philip had passed through many thrilling experiences since they had last met, and his story was rich.

At last, in response to a question, David admitted that the time had come for decisions and that there was a sense in which his was already made, but he did not yet know what his duty was nor whether he should take any outward stand in opposition to his own family.

He felt Philip's hand tremble on his arm. There was a strange solemnity in his voice as he said, " 'The one who loves father or mother more than me is not worthy of me.' I'm quoting *his* words, my friend, and I heard them under circumstances that will help me to remember them. My own people have cast me off utterly. My father will not even allow me to call at his house. I am practically homeless and friendless, so far as my own are concerned. Yet at times I can rejoice even over this. I don't need to speak to you of Frances. You will understand without words."

He could not keep his voice from trembling then, and David answered him only by a stronger pressure of his arm. Some sorrows are cut too deep for words. They walked on in silence.

Then Philip spoke again. "I mean that sometimes I can almost rejoice that I'm counted worthy to suffer with him. But I won't deny that the way ahead looks dark. Some of our number think the prophecy I've just been quoting from is rather figurative and is being now fulfilled; that a little ahead is brightness. They believe that men high in office are well founded in the distrust and fear with which they regard him; that he means very soon to set up his kingdom and give his faithful ones their immediate reward. But I have no such belief as that. What I have heard him say of himself does not justify it. What I see ahead is trouble and unutterable sorrow for him and his. Moreover, I believe we have enemies among us."

"You don't mean among his professed followers?"

"Yes, I do. We have one among us whom I utterly distrust. I had reason to in earlier days, and I see those same faults in him now. How can a man who is not honest in his dealings be trusted anywhere? Just what he means to do or can do, I don't know. But he will, as of old, bear watching. You know who I mean, of course? He is our treasurer. He has abundant opportunity, and I'm sure yields to temptation. Under other circumstances than those that exist now I should report him to our leader. But imagine my going to a man who has power to give sight to the blind and speech to the dumb, yes, even to raise the dead, and complaining to him of a fellowman! He evidently knows the hearts of each one of us better than we know ourselves. Yet he called this man to follow him and keeps him in our company. This is one of those instances when I ask myself why — and end up only in utter confusion."

When David reached his room that evening, he thought his next step was clear to him. He would seek an interview the following morning with the man he had determined to call 'Master' and ask for light as to his future course.

But he was doomed to bitter disappointment. He called as early as he thought courtesy would permit at the address Philip had given him and learned that the entire company had departed at daylight. The head of the house did not even know what route they had taken but had been told they would not return. The disappointed man could do nothing but give himself fully to the business that had called him there.

The usual unexpected delays occurred. It was much later in the season than David Holman had intended it to be when he at last presented himself again at the door of Miriam's home, only to learn that she was absent for the day. Her mother was profuse with explanations and regrets. Miriam had not received the note announcing his coming until that morning. Since she had arranged a riding party herself, she felt compelled to go. She regretted it exceedingly, of course, and wanted to take time to write a few words of explanation. But the others were waiting, and the mother had promised to say what was necessary.

David concealed his disappointment as well as he could and asked when he could see Miriam.

The answer was uncertain. "These moonlit eve-

nings are so charming to young people," the
mother said, smiling. "They're very apt to take
longer for these excursions than planned, and of
course Miriam can't hurry her guests. I'm really
afraid you'd better not plan to see her tonight. Tomorrow morning, of course, as early as you choose
to come, she'll be glad to see you."

Compelled to content himself with this, it did
not require much study to determine that he
would try to spend his leisure evening with Mr.
Rothwell. He could talk over questions of absorb-
ing interest better with him than with anyone else.
He escaped from Mrs. Brownlee and wrote a few
lines to his mother explaining a probable delay
longer than he had supposed. Then he went at
once out to the Rothwells' home.

There he found trouble. Mr. Rothwell was very
ill, and his sisters were absorbed in tending to him.
They greeted David as an intimate friend, and Mrs.
Symonds invited him at once to the sickroom. She
was anxious to know what he thought of their
brother's condition. Once there, it took only an
hour or two for David to prove himself the wisest
and tenderest of nurses, and his offer to spend the
day and the night was gratefully accepted.

Before the night fell, Mrs. Symonds was saying
between anxious sighs that she did not know what
they could have done without him. He seemed to
know exactly what to do for the sick man.

By morning David's resolve was taken. Here
was opportunity for him to repay some of the
many kindnesses the Rothwells had shown him.
The character of the illness was serious, and the
utmost care and watchfulness would be called for,
both of which he felt competent to give. He would
remain for a few days and devote himself to the

sick man. When he communicated his resolve to
the sisters, he received Mrs. Symonds's profuse
thanks and one swift look of gratitude from Mary's
eyes. David explained that he would have to go
into town to keep an engagement but would return
as soon as possible.

He found Miriam Brownlee in her prettiest
morning dress, delighted to see him and profuse in
apologies for yesterday.

"Wasn't it dreadful?" she said. "A genuine instance of self-abnegation. To tell you the truth, you
were to blame for it all. If you weren't so dreadful
about keeping promises and all that sort of thing,
I'd have broken mine and stayed at home to receive you. You can imagine how much I enjoyed
that day! Oh, David! It's so nice to think you've
come just now. We have several delightful young
people staying with us and no end of plans for
enjoying ourselves. We're going to the cascade this
evening by moonlight — you remember the cascade,
I hope? I'll be delighted to show it to you again.

"Your being here gives me just the opportunity I
wanted to include my sister Anna in the party. We
were to ride in couples and were short of gentlemen. And we have the most charming picnic
planned for tomorrow! We'll ride in single car-
riages out to Glen Avon — a long drive, you know
— and have a picnic dinner with a lawn dance afterward by moonlight. Won't that be lovely?

"It's an especially full week on account of these
friends of mine, who're to be here but a short time.
But we can manage to see a great deal of each other
at the same time. I'm sure you'll enjoy it. You've
been a hermit for so long that I'm charmed with
the idea of putting you back where you belong.
You've come to stay the entire week, haven't you?"

CHAPTER XXIII

HOPE DEFERRED MAKETH THE HEART SICK

h, poor David! How certainly there were two worlds, in one of which Miriam had made her life. How utterly out of character with the earnest words he had to say to her were picnics and moonlight dances and all the belongings of her world! How was he in a few sentences to explain to her that he did not belong to it? His continued silence finally arrested Miriam's attention. She studied his face closely.

"What have you been doing with yourself?" she asked. "You don't look well. I don't believe you slept at all last night. Where did you stay? I was vexed with Mama for not insisting upon your staying with us. Do you have a headache this morning?

Why are you so pale?"

"You're right," he said with a slight smile. "I didn't sleep last night. I watched with my friend Mr. Rothwell, who is very ill indeed. As no suitable attendant can be secured, I've promised to return to him as soon as I can — so the moonlight ride must be taken without me after all."

Miriam's face flushed, and her words came rapidly. "I'm sure I can't understand why. You certainly are not a professional nurse. What possible claim can the Rothwells have upon your services? I shall not consent to any such arrangement, I assure you. I planned the ride this evening with a special view to our having an opportunity to visit together, and I'm not going to give you up to watch with anybody."

"I beg your pardon," said David. "You evidently don't understand the situation. I went to see Mr. Rothwell on business and found him very ill indeed and needing the sort of care that his sisters are unable to give. Of course, I offered to stay with him until something better could be done, and of course you wish me to be true to my word."

"I don't know how I can be expected to wish any such thing. Your word doesn't always seem so precious to you, does it? How long is it since you promised to return to see me on purpose? When you were here before and gave these new friends of yours all your time, I didn't interfere, although I considered myself treated very strangely. But if the experience is to be repeated, I warn you that you'll find it difficult to make a satisfactory explanation."

David passed his hand wearily over his forehead and felt bewildered, but he kept his voice gentle. "Indeed, Miriam, I try to keep all my pledges. I explained to you how that was, and my letters have been full of regret for my long delays. But this is a very plain case — a friend is ill and needs me. When your cousin John was ill, did it seem strange to you that I watched with him night after night?"

"It was a very different matter," she said sharply. "John is my cousin, almost my brother. But the Rothwells are nothing to either of us. A mere business acquaintance you have known only a few weeks — yet you plan to put his interests before mine! Do you call that proper treatment of me?"

He stood before her utterly bewildered. He was really too high-minded to understand her insinuations. After a moment he made another attempt.

"I must be very stupid this morning. Have I explained to you that Mr. Rothwell's illness is critical and that proper professional care cannot at present be secured? I came to him providentially in the very hour of his need. I feel sure, Miriam, that when you take in the situation, you'll see that I couldn't do otherwise than I have done."

Apparently while he talked Miriam's mood changed.

"Oh, well," she said with her light laugh, "don't let us quarrel. If you must be spared to turn nurse today, why, I suppose you must, though the David Holman with whom I used to be acquainted would have given up all the sick men in the country for an hour of some people's society. That's nonsense, of course. You needn't look so shocked. But I am dreadfully disappointed. I release you then for the day. But remember that for the picnic and the dance you are engaged, and I shall take no excuse. They must find their professional nurse by that time."

He was not making progress. He was even posing under false pretenses! More than the illness of a friend was keeping him from this round of fashionable amusements planned out for him.

How was he to make plain to Miriam that he had reached a solemn epoch in his life — that grave sacrifices were before him, even that of being shut out from his own home and his mother? Above all, how was he to tell her of the hope he had indulged that he could convince her to sympathize with him? Clearly she was not in the mood this morning for such explanations, but — would she ever be? Ought he to wait and go away leaving her to imagine that he would carry out with her the exhilarating program she had arranged?

He arose abruptly from the seat beside her and walked the length of the pretty parlor. Then he pushed the only substantial chair in the room in front of her and sat down.

"Well!" exclaimed Miriam brightly. "You look formidable now in my grandfather's chair! Are you comfortable? You don't appear so. What's to be done next? Am I to have a sermon?"

He tried to smile in response to her raillery, but his words were serious enough. "May I not talk to you a few minutes about what fills my heart? If you'll let me, I think I can make my position plain. In any case, it's my duty to try. Miriam, the stranger of whom you and I have spoken before has come into my life with power. I have seen and talked with him and have made my decision. I accept him as my friend, my teacher, my guide in all things. All that he is to do with me and for me I don't know, but I have deliberately placed myself in his hands. Henceforth there is a sense in which I belong to him. All interests contrary to those which he plans must be put aside.

"This decision has already cost me much. My father is violently opposed to it all, and my home will probably be closed against me. Still I have made my choice.

"These are not the words in which I had hoped to explain to you, Miriam. But others will not come at my bidding. It seemed due you that I should speak without further delay. I know I've hurt you, but I must not be false to myself even to avoid giving you pain.

"Before you speak, let me add one sentence. I am absolutely sure that you are mistaken in your views of this stranger. You have been told many false things about him. You think his leadership includes interests which I do not believe it touches. If you'll trust me, Miriam, I will do nothing that will involve you in notoriety or be unpleasant to the most refined and womanly ideas. And I will introduce you to a friendship that is sweeter and purer than any earthly tie. Oh, the life that you and I together can live, if you will but let me show you what this means! May I tell you —"

He stopped abruptly.

Miriam had heard all that she would. She drew back the hand he tried to take and pushed her chair farther from his, and her voice was harder than he had ever heard it. "I call this very strange conduct indeed! The David Holman I used to know was a gentleman. This one has evidently adopted another code of rules from those which govern polite society. It is but a short time since you of your free will renewed the understanding between us and the one to which I had held myself true during all those years of your illness.

"No sooner, however, was this done than you

began a series of bewildering acts. Though I have the right to claim at least a portion of your time, I saw almost nothing of you. You came to the city where my home has always been and for an entire week did not call upon me. Of course, you were immersed in business; yet it gave you opportunity to attend services daily. All this I have tried to overlook and have received you as though nothing had occurred to hurt me.

"Finally you present yourself to me to report as a professional nurse, engaged to attend the brother of your new friend, and then pour into my ears the most astonishing statements I ever heard from a sane man's lips!

"You have resolved to cut yourself loose from family and respectability and follow the fortunes of an adventurer against whom I myself have warned you. I have told you that I knew, better than I could explain, the absolute danger in having anything to do with that man. I hazarded political secrets of no little importance to do so, all to no purpose.

"You have actually reached the point where you dare to ask me not only to tolerate you in this senseless and insane decision but to follow you in the life to which it will lead! You've gone too far! Once for all, you must choose between us. Either cut yourself free at once from all entanglement with this man and his friends, or don't presume to think of me as a friend of yours."

David had partially shielded his face with his hand and sat through these angry sentences in utter silence. When Miriam paused for breath, there was still silence for a moment.

Then he sat erect and looked steadily at his companion. "Miriam, one word. I would have chosen a

different time and different words for the revelation, but now it must be made. I believe with all my
soul that the man you call an adventurer is the
promised Savior of the world, come to us as a man
among men, that he may reach our inmost lives
and our deepest experiences. Believing this, could
I do other than I have?"

Instantly Miriam arose, a curious mixture of anger and fear in her face. She spoke low and rapidly:
"David Holman, the blasphemy you have uttered
is not new to me. I've heard of it before. In my
opinion there are only two classes of people who
make it. One class is deceivers, who know best
themselves what they hope to gain by such folly.
The other class is stark raving mad and ought to be
sent to a lunatic asylum without further delay. I
know you well enough to believe that you belong
to the latter class — and I'm afraid of you! I don't
say you are insane on any other subject, but I must
explain to you that until your reason returns to you
I do not want to see you again. It has been a humiliation and a disgrace to have my name associated
with yours since this mania took possession of
you, and I am resolved to endure it no longer. Oh,
David Holman! To think that it should have to
come to this!" Then she turned and hurried out of
the room.

For several minutes David kept his seat, his
head bowed in his hands. He could not think that
this was the end. He was sure that Miriam was not
afraid of him and had not for a moment thought
him other than sane. It could not be that she had
gone to stay. In a few minutes she would return to
say that she had been too hard and in a moment of
passion had spoken words she did not mean. He
waited and *waited*. Miriam had received him in the

small back parlor with the curtains drawn close
between him and the larger room. He waited until
callers came, asking for Miss Brownlee — gentlemen callers. He waited until the servant who had
received their cards came back to say that she
would be with them presently. Then he quietly let
himself out and walked down the street like one in
a dream.

Instinctively his mind returned to that dark
morning when he lay on his back and stared the
awful future in the face; he believed that life meant
for him just lying there and waiting for a coffin and
a grave. He remembered that the fiercest agony of
pain with which his soul did battle then was the
giving up of Miriam Brownlee. How many times
was he to be called upon to fight the same battle,
bury the same hopes?

It was better for him that the next few days held
him so closely to serious duties and responsibilities as to afford no time for thought about his own
interests. Mr. Rothwell's illness assumed a still
more alarming form as the days passed. The professional nurse had been secured, but the sick man
clung with the persistence of a diseased brain to
David; therefore he stayed.

Certain business interests, he discovered, could,
in the intervals of attendance upon his friend, be
looked after, thus aiding both Mr. Rothwell and his
father. This feature of the trouble his father could
appreciate, and daily letters passed between father
and son concerning the business complications re-
sulting from the illness of the chief. In the meantime, as the danger increased, the hearts of the
anxious sisters began to turn more and more toward their absent friend. "If he were only here!"
was the phrase now constantly on their lips. David

echoed the wish.

"If we could only get word to him," said Mary one morning, when their fears were at the highest, "I am sure he would come."

"But he went from here on account of the conspiracy against him," David reminded her. "Would it be safe for him to return?"

"I don't know," said Mary. "He would know. Some trusted messenger could go quietly to ask it of him — one who would hunt for him and yet make no public inquiries."

"Yes," said David after a thoughtful pause, "I could do that. I wonder that I've not thought of it before. If I can slip away from your brother without exciting him too much, I will make the effort."

She looked the gratitude her voice could not speak. After a moment she said simply, "I am almost sure he would come. He loves my brother."

Within an hour David was on his way. A long and perilous ride, sometimes along a mountain footpath where there was hardly room for the foot of a horse. But David, who in his boyhood had been familiar with almost every bridlepath in the country, had less difficulty in making his way than many others would have found.

It was on the afternoon of the third day that Mary, watching from an upper window, came to meet his return.

"He is still living," she said in response to David's look. "Oh, Mr. Holman! Did you not find *him*?"

"I found him, yes. Is there no change in your brother, Miss Rothwell?"

"Not for the better. I think the doctor has given up hope. Won't you tell me what he said?"

David waited to fasten his horse before he answered. He seemed to dread his task. At last he turned toward her: "Miss Rothwell, I have no word for you. He said nothing. Just at evening I reached the village where he is stopping and found my friend Philip Nelson, who took me to him. He was surrounded as usual by people of the poorer class, teaching and helping them. I made my way to him at once and gave him your message. Miss Rothwell, I don't know how to tell you that he seemed to have no interest in it. He was as one who had not heard. And yet I know he heard. Perhaps you will understand, though I don't, why a strange feeling should have come upon me just then that I must not question him. I turned away and came back as I went — alone."

"I am afraid I understand," said Mary Rothwell, her face very white. "It means that my brother is to die. Oh, Mr. Holman! Isn't it bitter, *bitter*, to have one's last hope taken away?"

"No," said David eagerly, "don't say that. He's not like any other, remember. Perhaps all the while he intends to come and knows that he will be in time."

Some such hope as that stayed with them all the next day. They took turns in watching from the eastern window the mountain footpath down which the Deliverer might come. They watched in vain. At sunset of that day the struggle was over, and the idolized brother lay robed for the grave. Even then they watched the footpath down the mountain. Could they forget John Brownlee?

"He met them on the way to the grave," Mary Rothwell said, searching Mr. Holman's face for some answering hope to her thought.

"Yes," he said, "and without being sent for. They had done what they could to keep him away. Don't give up the hope, Miss Rothwell."

Perhaps the burden was heavier because of this long-drawn-out agony of suspense. And they hoped in vain. The weary hours dragged themselves away, and all those terrible "last things" were lived through. The barriers of the grave closed over Mr. Rothwell's body, and in the deserted home the sisters wept alone.

CHAPTER XXIV

SHALL THE DEAD ARISE AND PRAISE THEE?

lthough there was no further need for watching, one of the watchers could not bring himself to leave the desolated house entirely. David Holman took a room in a hotel in town and spent most of the daylight hours at the Rothwell homestead. There was eminent reason for this. And it was, of course, eminently proper that Mr. Holman, whose father was connected with the same business, should be the one to take charge of the business matters so suddenly deserted by their chief.

The season was at its height, and a responsible head was most important, so the sisters could only express their grateful thanks to David for this added kindness. He saw almost as much of them as if he had been of the family, and he was evidently the one of all their friends on whom they were disposed to lean.

They talked together about many things but were silent concerning that one which lay heavily on the hearts of all. Why had the friend on whom their eager hopes centered utterly failed them? David was by no means anxious to break the silence; he felt disappointed and bewildered. If in his wisdom the Master had determined not to come to their aid, why had he not at least sent tender messages and assurances of unfailing love? Instead, had he not himself seen him turn from the news with an unmoved, almost an indifferent, face?

One evening Mary Rothwell suddenly voiced her thoughts. "Ours has been a strange experience. I could quiet my heart with the thought that my brother is needed in heaven, if only our friend had come to us and told us so, or sent us at least one comforting word. It is very, very strange, but it must be right."

"Yes," said David, holding back a sigh, "we must give him at least the consideration that we do other friends. When we cannot understand their acts, we can believe that their intentions were right."

"He does not make mistakes," answered Mary Rothwell. She arose at once, as though no more words could be trusted then.

Mrs. Symonds was not so reticent. She openly declared that she had not expected such treatment — so fond as he had been of their brother and so intimate in their home. It was all perfectly unaccountable.

The fourth day after the funeral David Holman was in the grapery directing some delicate work, when Mrs. Symonds came to the entrance and motioned him to her.

"Couldn't you go in for a little while," she asked, "and help poor Mary? The room is full of callers — people who have come to comfort us, poor fools! I bore it as long as I could. Mary is doing her utmost to make them all feel that they are kind. If you could go and do some of the talking, I know it would be a relief."

David signified his willingness to help in any possible way. Waiting only to give certain directions to the men, he went to his new duties. He was very slightly acquainted with a few of the guests; others he had not met. But he forced himself to take the lead in the conversation and was repaid by a swift glance from Mary's eyes which he could interpret and by her lapse into almost total silence.

Presently, fully engaged as he was and with every sense on the alert to ward off direct appeals to Mary, David still became aware that something unusual was going on outside. A boy dashed up the walk, ran around to the side door and held a conversation with someone, presumably Mrs. Symonds, for she almost immediately ran down the road in the direction from which the messenger had come. David carried on his divided train of thought and kept talking.

After a brief absence, Mrs. Symonds returned almost on the run and from the next room summoned Mary. The call was low. But Mary, seated near the door, evidently heard it and, without any attempt at explanation, arose quickly and vanished.

In a very few minutes thereafter both sisters hur-

ried down the walk. David regretted that one of
the callers had changed her seat for one near the
window; she now reported this singular action by
the sisters.

"Poor creatures!" said another. "How utterly
broken down they are. It is no wonder, I am sure.
They depended so entirely on their brother."

"I suppose they have gone to the grave," said
the friend by the window. "They headed in that
direction."

Then an energetic woman spoke. "How nervous
Mrs. Symonds is! She can't control herself as well
as Mary can. I declare, I tremble for her, lest her
brain will give way. Don't you think some of us
ought to walk down that way? It seems cruel to
leave those two poor things there alone. Some of us
who are best acquainted with them might follow at
a distance. Don't you think so, Mr. Holman? Or
perhaps you might go to them? I do hate to have
poor Mary left alone to look after her sister; she
seems so very nervous today."

Thus appealed to, David admitted that he was
afraid some news had come to the sisters to trouble
them. It was not their habit to hurry away in this
manner. If the friends would excuse him, he would
see if help was needed.

This was the signal for the callers to take leave.
To David's annoyance several of them followed
him at what they probably thought was a "respectful distance."

What he saw, as he passed the line of trees that
had obscured his vision, set his heart to beating in
great bounds. Just a few steps away, surrounded
by his immediate followers, was the man for
whose coming they had longed and prayed. At his
feet, in a perfect agony of weeping, was Mary

Rothwell.

David, as he drew near, heard her sob out her pitiful cry: "Oh, if you had been here, my brother would not have died!"

The face of the man who listened was full of sympathy and sorrow. He asked to be shown the way to the spot where they had laid his friend. Before they reached it, his tears were mingling with theirs. David, keeping in the background, was able to overhear much of the undertone of talk. Their followers had largely increased. Evidently it had been noised through the streets that the mysterious friend of the family had arrived, and curiosity seekers could not hold themselves away, even from a grave.

"Look at that man!" one observed. "The tears are rolling down his cheeks. They say he was very fond of poor Mr. Rothwell. Why didn't he come, I wonder, and try to cure him? Whatever they say of him, he really has performed some wonderful cures."

Suddenly all voices were hushed.

The sisters and their friend had reached the grave, and his hands were clasped as for prayer. "Father," he said, "I thank You that You have heard me. I know You always hear me. But because of the people who stand by I said it, so that they may believe that You have sent me." Was ever prayer like that heard at a grave before? There was no mention of the mourning ones nor any hint of their need for comfort in their great affliction.

The listeners looked at one another, startled, shocked. But if the prayer had astonished them, what shall be said of the next act of this mysterious man?

Advancing toward the grave, he spoke in a clear,

calm voice, not to any of the people gathered about, but to the silent occupant of the tomb. His words were a brief, authoritative direction to come forth. Then the awestricken people broke, some of them into screams of uncontrollable terror. Some ran from the spot, while others dropped in dead faints. At that voice of command a movement was distinctly heard in that quiet house where death was expected to reign until the judgment day, and the man whom they had laid away in the grave came forth and stood among them!

Of what use for a common pen to try to describe the scene in the Rothwell home that evening when the reunited family gathered for their evening meal?

"Have you written to Frances?" Philip Nelson asked his friend David the following morning, as they stood bidding each other good-bye.

"No," said David, "I have written to no one. I can't. There are some experiences that cannot be put into words. But I'm going home tomorrow. I shall try to tell her."

Meanwhile, in some respects a stranger scene than that which took place at the grave was being enacted in the city near at hand. A hastily called meeting of the leading men was being held, and prominent among the speakers was Felix Masters. He had taken it upon himself to set forth the dangers and difficulties of the situation.

The strange man who had been wandering over the country for many weeks had now succeeded in rousing the people to the very highest pitch of excitement by his last act. It was not to be denied that the man possessed some power by which he accomplished that which had been heretofore beyond human skill. But there was not the slightest doubt about its being power for evil — a power which, if allowed to be used undisturbed, would turn their cities and their homes upside down. The entire country was in danger. What the man was after was undoubtedly power of another kind than that which he now exercised. He meant to rule. What would the leaders think of themselves if they sat with folded hands and allowed this stranger to hypnotize the hearts and brains of the common people until they arose in power and brought about an insurrection of the bloodiest sort?

Undoubtedly the hour had come for action. They all knew what was now claimed by the fanatics. This meeting had been called to see how best to meet the emergency with that promptness which the danger demanded.

The president of the council arose to respond to Mr. Masters's statement. His manner was quieter, and his speech less inflammable. Mainly he confessed himself to be in accord with the last speaker, although he by no means took so gloomy a view of affairs. Of course they were bound to arrest this tide of error and superstition by which the country was being flooded, and undoubtedly they would do so. The strange man had proved himself a dangerous enemy, and of course the country must be given the first thought. Still, he advised very careful management; no good could result from antagonizing the common people. Their excitement must be soothed, and their prejudices catered to in a degree, in order to prevent an uprising.

Other speakers followed, and many plans of action were discussed. All seemed to be agreed that the dangerous stranger must answer for his crimes with his life. But the exact way in which this should be accomplished was not determined. Further, a careful official eye should be kept upon him, and his arrest made so soon as it would be safe to do so. Yet the crime which was the occasion of this remarkable meeting was the restoring to life and health of a prominent citizen of their district who had been dead for four days! It is true that this seems perfectly incredible. But when one is simply recording well-authenticated history, what is one to do?

Felix Masters went away from the meeting by no means satisfied. He expressed himself gloomily when the next evening he visited the town near which the Holmans lived and took occasion to call upon them.

"There is too much talk and too little action," he said. "I am convinced that our policy of delay is dangerous. I find myself awakening each morning with a sense of relief that no positive upheaval of the country has yet taken place."

"Why, do you really fear an outbreak of any sort?" Mrs. Holman asked incredulously.

"Indeed I do. An outbreak such as it will be, participated in by the very lowest classes, will, I assure you, be something to dread. The apathy of the leading men is amazing. A few vigorous steps now and the whole affair would be crushed. But the time is coming when it will require the loss of hundreds, even thousands, of lives to put it down.

"One needs only to travel through the country as my friend Mr. Compton has been doing to see how this astonishing bit of treason is being worked up. The man is keen-brained and as wise as a serpent in his methods. Already some of whom we had reason to expect better of have fallen his victims. I assure you that I am astonished and appalled over our apathy in this matter.

"Now, having said so much, may I speak even more plainly, Mr. Holman? I came here tonight hoping to meet your son. I wanted to tell him that his name is being quoted by outsiders as one who upholds this proposed insurrection. It may all be gossip, of course. Still, he is intimate with that unfortunately conspicuous family, the Rothwells. And I'm told that he still meets on friendly terms with that young traitor Nelson, who used to be in our employ. It is dangerous business, Mr. Holman. As a friend of your family I wanted to assure him of it and beg him to take pains to state that he is not in any way in collusion with their schemes."

The father's face was very pale as he heard this warning, but he was not a man who cared to sit and listen to the criticisms of others upon his son. He replied with exceeding gravity, and also with marked coldness, that he believed his own position was well known but that it ought to be remembered that his son was a man, not a boy, and was responsible for his own opinions.

Mr. Masters hastened to explain that of course he understood all this, and his exceeding anxiety for their welfare must be his excuse for this friendly warning. He had thought it possible that young Mr. Holman did not appreciate the gravity of the situation. Then, having made the family as miserable as he could, he took his departure.

The following day brought David. As his father listened with interest to the admirable business plans he had been able to carry out, he told himself that David had fully as keen a brain as that puppy Masters and had as good a right to do his own thinking. At the same time, with admirable consistency, he coldly told his heart that David would have to choose between him and the strange craze which seemed to have partly turned his brain.

As for David, what he thought or what he had decided he kept to himself and gave his entire time, and apparently all his energies, to his father's business. This, however, was only because his present duty seemed to be to wait, holding himself in readiness for whatever the future had in store for him. So far as Miriam Brownlee was concerned, she had herself checked his way, since he was not to return to her until he disclaimed all interest in his new friend.

There was in the midst of his sadness a thrill of solemn joy in his heart as he recognized that this new friend was for time and eternity. In taking this stand, he believed that he fully realized the situation. He had kept himself posted as to what was going on in the world. As he was as firm a believer in satanic influence as was Felix Masters himself, he could only feel that the extraordinary opposition to a man who had not only opened the eyes of the blind, but actually raised the dead to life, was the influence of Satan upon their hearts. With his Scriptures before him open to the words "Then the eyes of the blind shall be opened, and the ears of the deaf shall be unstopped," in the light of the facts which were already blazing before them, what else was one to think?

In the meantime all efforts to arrest the disturber of the peace seemed to have been futile. He and his followers had gone quietly away again. But it was generally understood that this was only a lull before the coming storm.

Matters were in this state when David received a letter from Mr. Rothwell, inviting him to be present at a series of special services and announcing that their "friend" was to be with them. He knew of the conspiracy against him, "understands it, I think, better than we do," the letter said; yet he was coming. They, his friends, meant to rally closely about him and do for him what they could. Would David join them?

While David was still busy with his mail, his father asked if he had not noticed Mr. Rothwell's handwriting among his letters.

"Yes, sir," replied David. Without note or comment he passed the letter to him. In his own mind he had become settled that final decisions must now be made.

CHAPTER XXV

Lover and Friend Hast Thou Put Far From Me

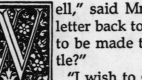ell," said Mr. Holman, passing the letter back to his son, "what reply is to be made to this remarkable epistle?"

"I wish to go, Father. I think I can arrange matters so that you will not need me especially for a few days. If you forward the letters, I can attend to them there."

"I will forward nothing!" interrupted his father, unable to keep his indignation within bounds. "Have you forgotten that I told you you must choose between your family and this adventurer? If you go in response to such a letter as that, you go not to return."

David's mother emitted a bitter cry: "Oh, Father,

254

Father! You don't know what you are saying. He is our boy, our only son!"

"I know very well what I am saying," the father replied, his features working painfully. "He is a son for whom I have sacrificed and suffered. And he is a son who chooses now to ignore all the past and separate himself from us for one who is an enemy to his country and a blasphemer of his God! He must make his choice; I am not driving him away. Even now I'm ready to forget what he has said and start afresh, as I believed that he had already done. But you all ought to know me well enough to understand that I mean what I say when I repeat that if David goes out from this house tomorrow with the avowed purpose of seeking that adventurer, he goes out not to return."

It was a terrible ordeal. If David could have forgotten his father, his mother's face of agony appealed to him. He spoke few words, and those very humble ones; but they seemed only to add fuel to the flame of his father's excitement. Yet the worst ordeal was to come. The mother sought her boy in his own room that night and pleaded with him for her sake to give up this folly.

"Dear Mother," said David, and he put all his soul into his voice. "Can't you understand that it is not for a passing fancy that I'm going? Mother, *God calls me.* To resist his teachings, to shut my eyes to the flood of light that he has sent me, would be the SIN of sins. Can you want me to do it?"

"How can you know this?" she asked, weeping. "How can you tell it's not a delusion of Satan as your father says? I wish with all my soul that it were not, and I cannot get my thought away from the hope — and yet — "

David had risen on his elbow and was regarding

her with a face which was strangely illumined.
"Dear Mother," he said. "Dear Mother, he is calling
you! I know it! I feel it! Mother, I have prayed for
this with all my soul. In his wonderful love he is
sending me the answer. Trust him, Mother. Pray to
him as your Savior. He will reveal himself to you.
Oh, I tell you I *know* that this is so!"

It was a strange interview, not at all as the
mother had planned. It lasted well into the morning hours. When she departed from him she knew
she had failed; in a few more hours he would leave
his home not to return. Yet she went away soothed
and comforted.

Crowding one of the broad aisles of the sanctuary were groups of people, pressing as near as they
could to hear the words of the strange teacher. It
was after the service. But he was lingering, talking
with them, and at the moment illustrating his point
with a story. Among the listeners were Mary Rothwell and David Holman. As the story progressed
they exchanged significant glances; they saw its
application very distinctly. So at the same moment
did Felix Masters, who with Miriam Brownlee beside him had pressed near enough to hear the
penetrating voice.

His face darkened, and he muttered something
that his companion did not hear. She had heard
little of the story. What had arrested and absorbed
her attention was the sight of David Holman. She
had been trying to determine just how much interest he felt in the fair girl who stood by his side and
who was apparently so absorbed in the speaker as
to have forgotten all others. Yet, when the two exchanged glances, swift intuition told Miriam that
whatever else they understood, they certainly un-

derstood each other.

The discovery was bitter to Miriam Brownlee. All her life she had been in the habit of ruling others. Not that she liked weak natures. The more determined they were in carrying out their own plans, the more she admired them, provided always that she could prove her influence stronger than any other.

By the same token, even while she had been angry with David Holman, she had gloried in his strength of character. Still she had expected him eventually to yield to her influence. It was preposterous to imagine that he would be entirely carried away by this strange infatuation, although she admitted that it had its fascinations. New ideas with an element of danger were always interesting, but he must not carry his interest too far. She had assured herself that rigorous measures were necessary, but she had had no fears as to the final result.

As the days passed, David seemed actually to be taking her at her word. He made no effort to see her again, and for the first time Miriam felt almost anxious. Was it possible that she might have gone too far? But that was absurd! David Holman belonged to her, body and soul — so she believed.

But on this day, when she stood watching him exchange significant glances with Mary Rothwell, she decided that she had been harsh and unjust. David, being a literalist, had taken her literally. She must take measures to have him understand that she had by no means meant all she said.

Watching for an opportunity as the crowd began to disperse, Miriam caught David's eye and smiled and bowed. He returned the bow but in a grave, preoccupied manner. She could almost have thought that he did not realize whom he was greet-

ing. Evidently he had no thought of crossing to her
side. She had supposed that recognition from her
would bring him. Now he really must come. When
their eyes met again, she gave him a very slight but
unmistakable summons. He looked surprised but
turned at once to Mary Rothwell.

"Miss Brownlee is motioning me to come to her.
Will you wait here or walk with me in that direction?"

She preferred to wait. Promising to return to her
in a moment, he crossed the aisle. Miriam greeted
him as though they had parted but the day before
and added in significant tones, "David, I want to
see you quite alone. When may I?"

He looked at her almost in bewilderment. For
the past few days he had been entirely absorbed
with interests of grave importance and with the
shadow of coming events; he only vaguely understood that in a sense Miriam Brownlee had passed
out of his life.

"Let it be this evening, if possible," she urged.

He replied quietly that he would be at the service that evening.

Miriam had intended to demand imperiously
that he spend the evening with her. She changed
her mind. "Very well, then, I will meet you here,
and we can talk on the way home as well as after
we reach there. Will you come and sit with us during the service?"

This invitation he declined; he had arranged to
remain with his friends. Then still with that preoccupied air about him he bade her good morning
and returned to Mary Rothwell.

Miriam Brownlee was inwardly surging with
passion. What did the man mean? He had been
almost insulting! If she could only be sure that his

dignified, preoccupied air was assumed for effect, she would promptly show him that two persons could play at that game.

While they were seated for the evening service, David had a view of Miriam's face as it was raised to the speaker's with an air of interest. There came into his heart a sudden great hope that she had at last felt in her own heart the power of the man and would be willing at least to listen carefully to his remarkable experience. What if both his mother and Miriam could be won? Yet even then he was preoccupied and thought of winning her only for her sake, not for his.

"It is a long time since we've taken a walk together, David. I didn't think you would treat me so!" It was Miriam's voice, as sweet and gentle as of old, but certainly with reproach in it, as they made their way following the evening service.

The bewildered David answered kindly. "I don't understand. You gave me no alternative. Do you remember what you said to me?"

"No," she said, "I don't think I remember very well. And you ought not to. I never supposed you were vindictive, David. Don't you know that I was so excited and frightened that morning that I did not realize what I said? My one thought was to save you from what I knew would be danger. I did not imagine that you would be so cruel as to translate my words literally."

He was very much confused. He hesitated as to how to word a reply. An embarrassed silence followed. Then he said, "I certainly believed, Miriam, that you spoke truth to me and that I was in honor bound not even to call upon you again unless I gave up what I knew I could never give up. What other course was there for me than the one I have pursued?"

Despite Miriam's effort to keep her voice sweet, a sting was evident in her words. "It seems to have been a very easy course for you. I cannot help but feel that you have been readily consoled. We are certainly different, David. There is nothing that I would not do or give up doing for your sake, even though I knew at the time that it was wrong."

Certainly they were different! He felt the truth of her words. Morally they seemed to live in different planes of thought. Or else — which of her sentences did she mean? He did not know how to talk to her, and another embarrassing silence ensued.

"You don't mean that, of course," he said at last. He resolved to avoid all personal conversation for the time being and began to tell her of some of the week's remarkable occurrences which were connected with the One who had become the focus of his thoughts. Since she had not meant her prohibition regarding him, it was fair to suppose that she might be interested in what he had to tell her, especially as it so intimately concerned him.

She interrupted him. "David, you expect me to listen to your story, but will you give no heed to my words? Don't you know that Mama is connected with people who can keep her well posted as to what is going on in official circles? When I risk my own interests to try to explain to you that great danger is in store, not only for that man, but for his adherents, why won't you be warned before it is too late?"

The very quietness of his tone irritated his companion. "I understand perfectly, Miriam. I know much more about it all than you imagine. Don't think me ungrateful for your efforts. But what I want you to know — what it is absolutely neces-

sary for all my friends to know and understand —
is this: I am fully committed to this man's cause. I
am ready to sacrifice position, home, life itself if
need be, at his call. There are worse experiences
than death; dishonor would be worse to me. I am
pledged to follow the lead of this man, even
though it may lead to imprisonment and to what is
worse than death — the loss of all my earthly
friends. *I mean the pledge.* I am in very solemn earnest. If I knew to a certainty that unless I retracted
at once from the position I have taken, my life
would be forfeited before morning, my life would
have to go. So entirely am I his that I would account it as a very little thing if it could prove my
loyalty to him."

He could not see the flush of anger on the girl's
face. With a strong will she held herself back from
the temptation to tell him that he was doubtless
consoled by the thought that he would not lose all
his friends; apparently Mary Rothwell was as insane as he. Instead, trying to speak lightly, she
said, "Very well. You must learn by experience, I
guess. I should have thought you would have
found it a bitter teacher. The immediate future will
show you your folly. In the meantime, though, let
us be friends. You don't know, you never will
know, how you have hurt me — but never mind.
Let it pass. I forgive you. I will do my utmost to
save you from being injured while this insanity
lasts. You, on your part, must forget all that I said
that morning. Shall it all be as before? Speak
quickly, David — Mother and Anna are coming."

"Good evening," said Katherine Brownlee's
voice the next moment at his side. "We haven't
seen you for a long time."

He might have murmured a single monosyllable

to Miriam, but he did not. He simply said, "I will see you again."

He walked home in a tumult of confused and contradictory thought. He seemed to be plunged again into the midst of perplexities that he believed had been settled for him.

Yet the very next day they slipped so utterly into the background that he did not think of Miriam at all. Contrary to his expectations, he did not go to the service but remained all day at the Rothwells' in company with the One he now unhesitatingly called Master.

The records of that day are unwritten. Indeed, so far as my knowledge extends, they are untold. David Holman talked much about it afterward, but only to Mary Rothwell and her brother and Philip Nelson, who shared the day with him. What they heard and felt that day, they seemed never able to share with any who were not present.

One item of business claimed David's attention. He went into town and secured for his use rooms in an unpretentious house on a quiet street. He had been to look at them before and needed only to make the final arrangements. To this quiet retreat early in the evening of that same day he introduced Philip Nelson.

"This is your resting place also, my brother," he said, with a significant emphasis on that word *brother*. "When you want to get away from everybody, come here. Tomorrow I will see to it that you have a key for your own use."

For answer Philip turned and clasped his hand. "I may be glad of a place of shelter," he said in a subdued tone. "Some wonderful experience is coming — I do not know what. 'He was led as a lamb to the slaughter.' You and I have read those words many times. What do they mean? David, two or three times he has talked to us lately as though he was actually going to *die!* But of course he cannot mean what we do by that word."

There was a moment of distressed silence, then Philip began again. "I have fears that I cannot, or at least will not, mention to him. You remember the suspicions I told you I had of one of our number? They increase upon me. He has been in conference several times with those who are avowed enemies of our leader. Only yesterday, for instance, he was closeted with Masters. What can those two have in common? I don't know what he could do, yet I have a presentiment that he means mischief. What broken reeds to lean upon!

"What do you think we heard concerning two of our number? Actually planning to be made prime ministers or something of that sort when he sets up his government! Trying to get ahead of the rest of us, you see — and they had the face to go to him with it! What must he think of us all?

"With such sordid views as that, and such underhanded scheming to carry them out, what sort of a government can we have when it is set up? I am tired of people, David — ashamed of them. What must the masses be, when out of our little company — "

He stopped abruptly as though ashamed of his outburst, but David met it halfway.

"My brother, let me ask you a question: Why did he choose such men to follow him? He who knows all hearts? Were there no others? Are we all self-deceived, unworthy to be trusted?"

Philip had no answer for him. He had thrown himself wearily back in a chair and was shading his face with his hand.

"I must go," he said suddenly, rousing himself, as a clock in the distance chimed the hour. "We have an appointment with him for the evening. Are you going to spend the night here? Then — may I return here? I want to talk some matters over with you. Don't wait for me. Don't even expect me. I may not be able to come. I don't plan for an hour ahead in these days."

CHAPTER XXVI

SMITE THE SHEPHERD, AND THE SHEEP SHALL BE SCATTERED

he first hint of a new morning was gathering in the eastern sky when David Holman was roused from sleep by the sound of footsteps. He had not gone to bed in his usual manner but had thrown himself fully dressed on the couch. The day had been so entirely unlike any other in his history; it seemed fitting that the night also should be marked by the unusual. Moreover, a vague unrest — born, he told himself, of Philip's words — had possessed him. He had left his door unlocked and had expected to watch for Philip's coming. He sprang up now to greet him. But even the dim light in the room revealed a face so haggard, so full of misery, that he could only exclaim,

"What is it, Philip? What has happened?"

There was no attempt at reply. Philip sank down on the foot of the couch in a miserable heap and buried his face in his hands. His friend bent over him anxiously, using the strongest incentive for speech that he could think of.

"What is it, Philip? Remember I, too, am anxious. If you *can* speak, I know you will not keep me in suspense."

Thus urged, Philip, without lifting his face, murmured, "It is all over. He has been led away like a common criminal, followed by a mob! They are at this moment going through the farce of an examination. Do you need to be told what the verdict will be?"

David's face grew white, and his voice was husky. "Aren't his friends permitted to be with him?"

But that question seemed to open afresh the very floodgates of misery. Philip threw himself upon his face and groaned like one in mortal pain. David, bending over him, distressed beyond measure, could only wait for words.

"He has no friends!" came at length from the prostrate form. "We are all traitors! He is deserted! We, who have told him again and again that we would follow him even to death — and I meant it — oh, God, I meant it then! — and I ran away and left him!"

"You don't know what you are saying, Philip. The night has been too much for you. You could never desert a friend."

David spoke as soothingly as he would to a child made insane with sorrow. He believed that Philip was in the delirium of fever. But his words seemed to rouse a perfect frenzy of remorse.

"I tell you," said Philip, sitting erect and glaring at him with wild eyes, "we have run away and left him to his enemies! That wretch, that traitor of whom I told you, led the way to the grove where we were meeting and pointed him out — and every one of us ran! Cowards and traitors! Those are his friends! All alike! You suggested the thought yourself last night, and here is the answer. Oh, that I could have done it!"

Of all the mornings of his pain-filled life, that one stood out to David Holman afterward as the most terrible. Knowing nothing of a certainty, with his heart torn by a hundred conflicting fears, he yet had to exert his utmost self-control and stay by the side of this man whom he believed to be out of his mind. Something had undoubtedly occurred, something of so terrible a nature as to dethrone his poor friend's reason. To desert him now would be worse than cruelty. He must wait and minister to him as best he could.

So it came to pass that the sun was hours high before the two men went forth together to watch that scene, which because of its unparalleled horrors, makes the day stand out from all others in history. Through all the years it has refused to be described by human pen.

The city was athrob. Apparently the rabble, so long dreaded by some, had taken possession, with no attempt on the part of the authorities to restrain them. The rabble was the sort that thirsts for excitement and is willing to sacrifice anything or anybody to have its awful appetite gratified.

The farce of a trial was carried out, with the inevitable verdict that could alone have been expected. It was pushed with insane haste — more like the haste of wild animals after their prey than

of men who were pretending to administer justice
— and it appalled even some of those who had
planned for this result.

Through it all the calm, serious man moved
among them as a king. Though sneered at,
mocked, struck and even spit upon by brutal men
in the jeering throng, his face never lost its dignity
nor its calm. The friends who had deserted him in
a sudden and awful panic which they could neither explain nor understand rallied again. They remained as close to him as the officials would
permit and were as powerless to help him as was
the dust under their feet.

As the hours passed, the ever-increasing crowd
seemed to grow more and more reckless. Some
power was at work feeding their evil passions.
Those who had received blessings at that man's
hands shouted the loudest that he was a traitor
worthy of death.

David Holman looked on utterly powerless and
utterly sick, trembling in every nerve at the
thought of the possible end. He wondered, as one
might wonder who did not belong to this human
life at all, whether Philip was right, and there was
no one anywhere to trust.

Where, for instance, was God that this awful
thing was allowed to be? His lips would not have
formed such words, but his poor brain tottered on
the very verge of insanity, seemingly determined
to force upon him the awful question.

It took hours to realize that they actually meant
to carry out the verdict pronounced after the greatest mockery of a trial that ever disgraced the
world.

When the terrible truth dawned upon them that
nothing was to be done to save their friend, they

gathered, his immediate followers, in little horror-stricken groups with no words to speak. They were few in number, most of them poor, and they had no political influence whatever. Mr. Rothwell, it is true, was wealthy; and there were others who would have been glad to give money, but to what end? They recognized its powerlessness. Of what use to clamor for justice, when it had been made glaringly apparent that justice was the thing to be avoided?

With every passing hour the horror seemed to deepen. Yet some of these strange men were up-held by an unreasonable hope that something would yet intervene to prevent the awful tragedy from reaching completion. What had become of the power which the man himself possessed? How certainly some of them knew that he possessed it! Could he not exercise it for his own preservation? If he could, would he?

The people, those dreadful people whose friend he had been, evidently believed that he could not. They taunted him with it.

"You saved others," they said. "Why don't you look out for yourself? If you can do that, we'll believe on you."

They were answered only by dignified silence. Throughout the entire awful scene, that majestic calm that ought to have spoken to them of king-ship never left him.

There came an hour when his friends sat, each wretched soul wherever one could find a spot alone, with a misery too deep for human eyes to behold, trying to convince their stunned hearts that it was all over. The friend, helper, healer, the One on whom they had rested their hopes, not alone for time but for eternity, was DEAD! Buried!

His life had been wonderful beyond all understanding. But it had ended like all lives — the
grave had closed over it! Their hopes were dead.
At least some of them reached this last abyss of
misery.

David Holman, after all was over, spent some
time in searching for his friend Philip. During
those closing hours of horror he had simply forgotten his existence. Failing in the search, he retired to
his rooms almost indifferent. What were human
friendships now?

Late at night Philip came. Poor David, seeing in
his face a greater misery, tried feebly to speak some
word of relief. What was there to be said? By degrees he heard something of those last hours they
had spent together. Philip, who had resisted all in-
vitations to lie down and take some rest, seemed to
find relief in talking.

"Don't speak of sleep to me," he said bitterly. "I
slept that night, when I might have stayed awake
and watched. Satan had possession of us all! And
we were warned, David. He told us that very evening that one of us would before morning deny
that we knew him!"

It was thus, in detached phrases, that David
heard the story. Every word added to his bewilderment. They had been warned, those twelve friends,
of a traitor in their midst. He had actually been
pointed out to one of them! It had not been understood then; it was plain now. Bit by bit the events
immediately to follow had been outlined for them,
and they had been too stupid to look at the picture.
Why did a man having such power allow such results?

From time to time, as they occurred to him,
David asked minor questions. "What has become

of that traitor?"

"He killed himself," said Philip. "And it is well
he did. It does not seem as though the same world
could have held us. But what am I to say to that?
He was only a degree or two beyond me."

"Hush!" David rebuked his friend sternly. "I
will not hear you malign yourself. No deeper-dyed
villain ever walked the earth than that traitor."

"There are degrees in vileness, I suppose," said
Philip gloomily. "But think of us curled into comfortable positions sleeping through those hours in
which we were set to watch! When I think of it all,
I long to die. As for my friends, they will be justified in never wanting to hear my name again."

David knew that he was thinking of Frances and
essayed to speak a word of comfort. "My poor
friend, you are too hard upon yourself. You were
utterly worn out that night, remember. Do you recall the two previous days and nights? No one will
think it strange that you dropped asleep."

"Nor that I ran!" said Philip in bitter self-denun-
ciation. "I know of but one poor wretch who may
possibly feel even worse than I. Three times he denied that he even *knew* his leader! But mine was
only denial in another form. Don't, David, try to
make me believe that I am other than the utter
coward, the worthless wretch that I am. I hate myself and always shall. I do not know how to bear
it!"

It was thus that they spent the night.

The morning broke in gloom. The sky was over-
cast with leaden clouds. That was well, for they
would not have had the sunlight mock their pain.
The city's excitement had spent itself, and everywhere quiet reigned. To those who had buried
their hopes, the day seemed to stretch out end-

lessly.

Philip refused almost fiercely to attend the service — what was it all to him now? So David went alone. He felt that if Philip could be by himself so that he could pray unobserved, he might get into a calmer mood. Also he confessed to his heart an anxious desire to hear from the Rothwells and find how they had borne the awful strain, as well as to learn what they thought would be the next page in their life's story.

To his great astonishment he met his sister Margaret in the hall of the sanctuary.

"Don't be frightened," she said, as she laid her hand on his arm. "Nothing terrible has happened. I am here visiting Miriam. I came yesterday with Mrs. Brownlee and John. David, you look as though you had had a fit of sickness! Miriam wants to see you very much. I promised her I would ask you to call upon her this afternoon. Will you?"

"I don't know," said David apathetically. He had a feeling that what he did made little difference now.

"Why don't you know?" questioned Margaret. "She is very anxious. Are you ill, David? I never saw one change so much in so short a time. I suppose you have been living on your nerves for the past few days. It has certainly been a horrible time. I feel thankful that it is all over."

"Don't!" remarked David sharply. "Do not talk about that, Margaret. You don't understand. If Miriam has a special reason for wishing to see me, I suppose I can call today, but — "

He made an abrupt pause. He had been on the verge of saying that he had no desire to see her. Did he mean it? He must not trust himself to further words.

"I think I will call," he said and entered the sanctuary.

The Rothwells were in their seat. Mr. Rothwell, motioning him to sit with them, asked if he would go home with them after the service for an important talk. Then Mrs. Symonds leaned forward and asked if that were not his sister in the Brownlee pew, and would he bring her out with him? They would like to know her.

"Dear me!" said Margaret, when this word was passed to her after the service. "Who imagined that such an event would ever happen to me? I believe I will go. I have heard more about that wonderful sister and brother than I have about any other people in the world, I believe. But, David, you said you would call upon Miriam this afternoon?"

Thus reminded, David sent word by Mrs. Brownlee that he would call later in the day. Mrs. Symonds and Mr. Rothwell took Margaret under their care, leaving him to walk with Mary. It was an opportunity that he had craved, and he eagerly seized upon it.

"I feel as if I have lived a hundred years since I saw you last and have passed through experiences that have all but wrecked me," he confided. "You have borne the same, yet your face does not indicate it. What do you say?"

"There is nothing to be said," she answered with the quietest of smiles. "We have only to wait — wait and trust. I don't pretend to understand anything, but I'm sure that he does."

"Then you do not feel that we were mistaken, deceived, that all is lost?"

"Mr. Holman! Deceived in *him!*"

"I do not mean just that," he said quickly. "I mean — have we not misunderstood him and indulged in hopes that were not justifiable?"

"No. Undoubtedly we don't understand him fully. But the hopes we have, he has inspired. He is to be trusted implicitly until he explains to us."

"But," David said with an uncontrollable tremor in his voice, "the grave has closed over him."

"So it did over my brother, Mr. Holman."

"I know — but — "

She interrupted him firmly. "No, I cannot talk with you if you speak in that way. There are no 'buts' in unwavering faith. How long he means to let the grave claim him I do not know. That he is alive, we surely know. That much faith we have for our ordinary friends whose bodies are buried out of our sight. That he is planning and controlling our lives today, I don't doubt any more than I doubt my own existence. What the immediate future may have for us, we must wait and see. Can you not trust him?"

There was a minute's silence, then he said firmly, "Yes, I can. Thank you, Miss Rothwell. I needed your faith to supplement mine. I felt like one lost in the dark, and dizzy." After that, he thought of his appointment with Miriam Brownlee with increasing discomfort. What could he say to her about these thoughts that filled his mind?

Meanwhile, he was thankful that Margaret had at last been brought within reach of Mary Rothwell's influence. She had changed in the few weeks they had been separated, or else she was showing another phase of her nature. The light, mocking laugh she had caught from Miriam was not heard once that afternoon. She was in the library with Mr. Rothwell for nearly an hour before dinner and seemed to listen with keen interest to what he was telling her. Would he be likely at this time to talk at length upon any subject save one?

David hoped a great deal from this visit. He was even more encouraged because Margaret chose to remain and accompany the Rothwells to evening service, instead of walking back with him when he went to keep his appointment with Miriam. It seemed to him that no one could be under the influence of Mary Rothwell, even for a single day, without being made better because of it.

CHAPTER XXVII

HE WILL SWALLOW UP DEATH IN VICTORY

iriam was in her most winning mood.

"My poor friend!" she said, detaining David's hand in gentle pressure. "My heart aches for you. I've longed for an opportunity to tell you how fully I sympathized with your crushed hopes. Now you know something of the fears I had for you, amounting almost to torture. I was afraid that some of that poor creature's friends might suffer with him. Can you understand me now better, David, than you did before you knew the danger?"

"I understand your meaning," he said with the gravest manner. "I understood the cruelty of our enemies better than you supposed, and I believed that some of us might be privileged to show our devotion by our lives. But that was not to be. We need not talk about it now."

"No," she said, "we need not talk nor think about it anymore. I am sincerely sorry for you, David, for I know what you must have suffered. Friendship, with you, means a great deal. But I will not deny that a great terror has been lifted from my heart. I cannot but be glad that the barrier that seemed to threaten *our* friendship has been removed. I knew the time would come when you would realize that you were following a delusion. But, oh, it was hard to wait, being afraid all the time that evil would touch you first. You do not wonder, do you, that I feel almost happy now that it's all over?"

Her smile was one that only a few weeks before would have thrilled him. He looked at her now in dumb surprise and felt as though his heart was dead.

"Can anyone be happy now," he said vaguely, "in view of the awful crime that has been committed?"

"I know," she admitted. "There was a most unnecessary cruelty. Don't imagine that I excuse it. I said all the time that it was horrid. Let us not talk about it. Such things are dreadful! Let's talk about ourselves. David, I've had to seem cruel myself, I'm afraid, in order to maintain self-control. Do you know, I had an awful fear that this matter might in some way separate us permanently? Besides, as a family we are so closely connected with the government that to have appeared in the least disloyal would have been dangerous. Oh, David! I am so glad that it is all over, and we need not waste our precious time together in talking about it anymore."

How was he to talk to this girl? All over! Could any words be more sharply contrasted than hers and Mary Rothwell's?

He answered, more because he must say something than for any hope he had of impressing her: "You feel that because a friend is dead and buried, all is over? Is death, then, a matter of such infinite importance?"

"Now, David," she said, leaning forward and placing her hand lightly on his arm in the old manner that used to be irresistible. "I don't mean to be unreasonable. A grave and a memory are sacred things. I do not mean to be jealous of either. But, after all, they are very different from a living — obstacle." She hesitated over the last word and smiled that old daring smile she used to have when resolved to speak words, whether they shocked or not. "You don't like for me to say that, do you? But he did come between us, David, cruelly. Can I be expected to mourn deeply the loss of one who did that?"

He could not talk with her! Every word jarred. And yet she was his promised wife! He had supposed that the bond between them was broken forever, but she had not understood it thus. However, she was still deceived. He must try to explain.

"No, Miriam, it was your decision that came between us. I was not to come to you again until I was convinced that I was following a false light. That time has not come and never will. That I am disappointed beyond words in the solemn change which the schemes of evil men have brought upon us, I will not pretend to deny. But that I have given him up or that I trust him less than I did last week or that I owe my allegiance less to him now than then, I also deny. The vows I took were for eternity and have nothing to do with death. You do not in the least understand what he was and is to me. There are times when I fear you never will."

"David!" she cried. "You are cruel! Have you learned from this new teacher not to forgive hasty words which were spoken in the excitement of terrible fear? I tell you I feared for your *life* and was trying to save you! I never meant to separate us, but only to force you away from an awful danger. Why should you talk to me in this way? Why shouldn't I understand your religious life? Am I not also a member of the congregation? What can you mean to do except to take a leading place in it as a man of your position and education should? And why shouldn't I be in utmost sympathy with all that?"

David rose abruptly. He had no words that fit Miriam Brownlee. To prolong the interview seemed impossible. To her earnest protest he replied that he could not talk longer, could not even think clearly. Some other time, as soon as his confused powers had rallied sufficiently for him to know what to say, he would try to explain to her what she was now very far from understanding — his beliefs and his future desires and plans. He ought not to have called yet. The blow upon him had come too recently. His faith was stunned, he told her with the most sober of smiles, but by no means dead. As soon as he knew how to tell her about it, she should see him again.

She looked after him with darkening brows as he walked rapidly down the street. She was disappointed and perplexed: Fanaticism has a deeper hold upon him than I imagined. But a leader in his grave is certainly not formidable. Who would have

believed that David Holman could be such a fool!
Yet he is more noble in his folly and more interesting than anyone I ever knew. I can afford to wait
until he rallies. But it is all very trying. These were
some of her thoughts as she watched.

As for David, he spent the remainder of that day
alone, as far away from people as a long tramp into
the country would take him.

"Though he slay me, yet will I trust in him" were
the words, among others, that floated through the
chaos of his brain. They recurred to him again and
again. The import of his thoughts may be gathered
by the fact that he said at last aloud and solemnly,
albeit there was no one near to hear: "Though he
has allowed *himself* to be slain, yet will I trust in
him. The Lord in his mercy help me to do so."

He reached the sanctuary after the evening service, in time to walk home with Margaret. To his
relief, she asked no questions about his interview
with Miriam. She was subdued and gentle.

As they neared her stopping place she broke
forth. "David, I want you to know how sorry I am
for you and that I do not feel as Miriam does. I'm
sorry I carried her message to you this afternoon.
I'm afraid she hurt you. She seems almost to rejoice
over the horrid cruelties that were permitted in the
name of the law. I didn't realize how dreadful it
was until I heard those people talk. If you feel as
they do, David, it must have been terrible. I think
you are all in terrible error, and of course you will
find that out now for yourselves. But it was a fearfully vicious way in which to learn it. I cannot understand why those in power permitted such
doings. Could nobody have helped it, David?"

"Yes," he said, "a word spoken confidentially in
the governor's ears by his nephew, Felix Masters,

would have done wonders toward staying some of the cruelty, and we have good reason to know that he threw his influence all the other way."

His words were fierce perhaps; he was not certain. But surely this was an opportunity to try to weaken that bad man's influence over his sister.

She was still for some seconds. Then she broke forth again. "David, don't you think Mr. Rothwell prayed tonight for those awful wretches who mocked at and spit upon his friend and even jeered while he was dying?"

"An example was set for him," said David, his voice husky with feeling. "In his deepest pain our leader said, 'Father, forgive them.' We must try to follow."

And then they were at the gate. David bent and kissed his sister's face and found it wet with tears. Shed as they had been for another's pain, they comforted his sore heart and gave him hope for Margaret. Miriam had had no tears to shed. Instead, her words had jarred even Margaret.

He waited late that night for Philip, who did not come. Then, sick at heart and weary almost of life, he threw himself fully dressed as he was upon the bed and fell into a heavy sleep.

He was roused by vigorous knocking at his door. It could not be Philip, for the door had been left unfastened for his sake. Following the knock came an eager voice: "Let me in, David, quick!"

David sprang from the bed. It was John Brownlee's voice. Something new had happened. But John's eager face had no terror in it. He was all but breathless with haste.

"Have you heard?" he asked. "Did you think any of the time that the grave could hold *him?* I didn't; and it hasn't! It is empty! He is here! They

saw him! Man! Do you hear me? He is alive, I say!
Why don't you shout? scream? Oh, I am crazy with
joy!"

David stared at his visitor like one in a trance.

"Do you know what you are saying?" he asked
at last.

"Do you know what you are doing — standing
there like a statue, when the most wonderful thing
that could happen *has*? David, I tell you that grave
is empty! The grave clothes are folded and lying
there in order. The One who wore them doesn't
need them! I think it is a wonder that the very
stones do not shout!"

Long afterward David wondered over his stu-
pidity that morning. That any of them could have
been so dull of comprehension seemed past belief.
But at the time he thought it was self-control.

"You are wild!" he said to John Brownlee. "My
dear fellow, these awful days have been too much
for you. Don't think for a moment that I have lost
faith in him. I believe that, for some reason which
we do not understand, he has chosen to die. But *he
is dead*. Don't let us make ourselves insane over
false hopes. Where did you get this story? Have
you seen Philip or any of them?"

"No," John said, his joy dampened a little by
David's quiet, firm tone. He had seen only some
women, his dear friends, and they had told him.

"Oh, 'some women'!" and David turned wearily
toward the couch and threw himself down again.
"That isn't strange. Those poor women with their
torn hearts cannot be expected to have clear brains.
But you and I are men. We must be brave and bear
up under this blow and help the others. We shall
see him again, my brother, but not here. He has
finished his work here, giving us all the opportu-

nity we needed, and now he has gone."

"I don't believe it!" said John Brownlee, and he dashed away again.

Poor David felt that this was almost too much. Surely he had borne enough without going through the ordeal of trying to help calm such a furor as this wild story would cause! He could not help — not until he was stronger physically. For the first time since his recovery he felt really ill.

Looking back over his past, he said afterward that that day stood out as one to be described in a single word: desolation. He left his room very soon and wandered about aimlessly, not meeting any of his friends and not trying to find them. Above all he avoided the road that led to the Rothwells'. He told himself that he had no excuse for intruding upon their sorrow. But deep in his heart he knew that he must not visit there anymore. Loyalty to what Miriam Brownlee believed was the situation must hold him away. He had believed himself free, but — he shrank from himself almost in horror as that "but" revealed to him a glimpse of his heart.

Was he then so little to be relied upon even as a friend? He declined to think further in that direction — not until he was rested. Before that weary day was done he thoroughly hated his own companionship and bitterly despised himself. He left the city far behind him and tramped all day until his body ached with weariness. But he could not get away from himself.

Twilight found him walking slowly toward his rooms. He dreaded to go back, dreaded the loneliness and dreaded Philip or, indeed, any of his friends, more even than he did solitude. He had besought John Brownlee to be brave, but every vestige of bravery seemed to have slipped from him.

He was dissatisfied with every suggestion that presented itself for doing away with the evening and felt sure that in his present mood he could not attend the little meeting that had been planned. He continued on with his eyes on the ground and presently ran into a man coming from the opposite direction. Mutual apologies ensued and then a recognition. They had met several times at Mr. Rothwell's and had been drawn toward each other.

They stood conversing together for a moment. Then David turned and walked in the gentleman's direction. The talk increased until both were so interested that David was urged to accompany his new friend home and spend the night; he lived but a short distance out of the city. David was easily persuaded. He had never felt more sorely in need of the right companionship. Besides, this man had heard the wild rumor of the morning, and he wanted to find out exactly what he thought about it.

"I confess that it has a strange appearance," the other said. "The grave is certainly empty, and the grave clothes were lying there folded, as though some person of infinite leisure had looked after them. Of course, our enemies must have had the body removed, but it has been done in an unusual manner. I haven't met any responsible person today. I saw several women who were insane with sudden hope, but of course — "

"Yes," said David, as though their hope was too preposterous to talk about. At that moment a stranger walking their way bade them a courteous good evening and, accommodating his pace to theirs, asked a question or two about the locality. Then he asked if he might inquire what had occurred in the city lately to cause great excitement and evident depression on the part of some.

"You must indeed be a stranger," said David's companion, "if you have not heard of the tragedy that has taken place in our city!"

Question and answer followed until they found themselves detailing the story to this stranger. David found it a relief to go over the particulars to one who, though a sympathetic listener, yet could listen quietly and seem not utterly crushed under the climax. As he talked he felt wonderfully drawn toward the man. He felt as though he could pour his very heart out to him as he had been able to do with no other. When he reached the story of the morning's report, he told it as though his poor heart was broken. Certain women had brought the strange report. It had even been wildly rumored that one of them had *seen* him! It had all served to emphasize their loss to them as nothing else had done.

"Ah, but," said the stranger, "it seems to me that you don't understand your Scriptures. Isn't there more than a hint there of many things that have taken place? What, for instance, does this mean?"

From that moment on he took the lead in the conversation, quoting verse after verse from the Scriptures with which these two had been familiar since childhood. Yet he shed a peculiar light upon it, insomuch that some mysteries were already made plain. They exchanged glances of astonished delight. As they neared their stopping place, David's host urged earnestly the hospitalities of his home upon the stranger. "I beg you will stop with us," he said. "It's growing late, and there is no good place nearby in the direction you're going. We should be very glad, my friend and I, to have you tell us more about your study of the Scriptures. We have heard nothing like it, and this subject interests us more deeply than any other. Won't you stop and help us?"

Thus urged, the stranger yielded, and they entered the house together. The table was spread, waiting for them. In a very few minutes they sat down for their belated supper. The stranger was invited to ask a blessing. He bowed his head — with the first word uttered came to David's heart its revelation. Not a question, not a possibility or a hope; simply a certainty! There was no other voice like that in all the world. They had been stupid, blind! It was the Master himself who had mercifully blinded their eyes to his visible self while he illumined their minds with his prophetic history.

CHAPTER XXVIII

I WILL WORK, AND WHO SHALL LET IT?

he days and weeks that immediately followed were filled with a series of experiences unparalleled in human history. The Master, as more and more of his followers delighted to call him, was with them again in the flesh. The almost delirious joy with which they had at first received the news settled after a few days into joyful assurance. So did the doubts that some who would fain have believed but could not, until evidence past all questioning was given them.

Yet they had a very different association with him now. He was the same kind, wise Friend and Guide, and he was something more. A strange awe grew upon the little company as they felt, rather than realized, the mysterious change. They could not make an appointment with their Leader quite as they had heretofore. They could not count upon the probabilities of meeting him at certain places. The bounds of the flesh which held other men seemed to have lost their power over this one. He appeared to them suddenly, unexpectedly, at times when they supposed him far away from them. They grew to understand that, no matter where he was known to be at one moment, the next might bring him before them.

The experience had its confusing side. His friends felt unsettled, in doubt, as to what was expected of them or how they ought to plan. The strange unrest that every one of them realized grew with the days. Why did they not boldly ask him what they should do? They did not like to own to one another that they were almost afraid of him, but what was the feeling that sealed their tongues? They who had been so ready to talk!

It chanced one evening that a number of them met on the lakeshore where they had spent so many pleasant hours with their Teacher. Every one of them was recalling with a vague sense of regret those precious past times, yet not one liked to refer to them. The present mystery rested too deeply on them for speech, even among them.

Suddenly one of them broke the quiet, speaking in his old light tone, like a man who had resolved to throw off solemnity. "I'm going fishing!"

They caught at it eagerly. "That's an idea. Let's all go. A row on the water will rest our brains perhaps."

They had been skilled fishermen in their very recent past, and with no little eagerness they prepared for a night on the water. Perhaps the unspoken thought of each was a desire to do something that would seem natural.

It was late when they started. They rowed and talked, and fished unsuccessfully, and were loath to separate. They let the hours wear away until the dawning of a new day began to tint the eastern sky, then they turned toward the shore.

"We have lost our skill," one of them said. He added, "Do you remember that the Master said when he called us that he would make us fishers of men? Perhaps we have failed in order that we may be reminded that our work lies elsewhere."

Dimly outlined on the shore was a man who seemed to be watching their boat with interest.

"Caught any fish?" The question rang out from the shore.

The brief answer was returned. "No."

Again came the clear voice: "Cast your net on the right side, and you will find some."

They looked their surprise at one another. Who should know these waters better than they? Yet there was such assurance in the tone that it was almost a command. They wondered why they should feel inclined to obey. Each did not like to admit to the other that he meant to. Yet they prepared to cast the net. Almost as soon as it touched the water it was aswarm with fish!

They gazed at it in awed silence, until one murmured low: "It is the Master!" Then with swift, silent work they gathered in the fish and made for the shore.

The night was gone. Morning was flushing the eastern sky, but the early air was chill. On the shore not only was a cheerful fire burning, but a breakfast was being prepared. Fish were already cooking on the coals.

No one was near save their Friend and Master. He had planned then for their comfort — had actually spread the breakfast for them!

"Come," he said in his old, kind, caretaking voice. "Come and dine." For the first time since he came back to them their hearts went out to him as their very own! And the terror they had sometimes felt about him passed away forever.

"In some respects it was our most remarkable experience," Philip Nelson said to David later. "Can you imagine what it was to see him watching us from the shore and to hear his kind voice calling us to come to the breakfast that he had himself prepared? Those commonplace words reminded us of his full knowledge of our everyday needs and helped us beyond all telling.

"Ah, but, David, I wish you could have been with us and heard his talk afterward! I cannot even try to repeat much of it. It would be a breach of confidence to do so. It was especially for that one of our number who needed it most. Yes, I mean the one who denied that he knew him. David, we must none of us think of that anymore. The Master has forgiven him and blessed him. Oh! He will no doubt tell you about it himself. But it is for him to do, not for us. Indeed, the more I think about it, the more I realize that he fell because he dared to follow at a distance. He thus had opportunity to be tempted, while the rest of us slunk away out of danger. But the way the Master has treated it is another proof of his immeasurable love."

After they had gone over every detail again and again, and his hungry soul had taken every crumb that Philip was willing to give, David said, "Well, what next? What are we to do? What is it that he wants of us?"

"We don't know," said Philip. "The day has evidently passed when we can question him as we once did. There is no mistaking the change, brother. He is Friend, Helper, Leader, just as before. But he is also King. We must bow before him and wait. For the first time in my life, David, I am willing to wait."

In the meantime, those officials who had risen in their strength to rid the world of this dangerous man professed to have only smiles or sneers for the ignorant few who were still trying to cling to their delusions. Without leadership, they said, these were but harmless lunatics that time would cure. What they actually thought, it would be difficult to tell. The little band of faithful ones knew they were under surveillance and could not even gather for prayer without being closely watched. In those and other ways the officials plainly showed confusion and consternation over the result of their work.

Whoever else had doubted for a time the story of that untenanted grave, the officials had not. The grave had been guarded by a band of soldiers so there could be no possibility of the body's being carried away by friends. These soldiers were brave men, thoroughly armed, and feared no human foes. And the story that they told about the grave was simply beyond belief!

Yet what was to be believed? The dead man — none knew better than they that he had been dead — was said to be abroad again in the flesh!

The lives of these men during those days need not be envied. They had shown their ability to cope with an enemy in the guise of a poor unarmed man without influence among the great and powerful. But an enemy who moved among them unseen, yet whose power was felt and realized; who was constantly heard of here and there and seen and talked with by those he chose to meet; yet who walked their streets and spoke in their religious gatherings no more; who had no more to do with those who had not enrolled themselves as his followers; who could never by the most intense vigilance be found; who disappeared utterly just at the moment when they thought they had him again within their grasp — all this filled them with a strange terror that it would have been fatal to have admitted.

The little company of chosen ones kept their own council. As the days passed, their faces gave occasion for more perplexity. They seemed to be anxious no longer. All sense of unrest had departed. Instead, they appeared to be joyfully expectant. What would be coming next, and how would those wise leaders cope with it?

Six wonderful weeks — the annals of which, if they could be written, would make a book the like of which the world has never seen — passed all too swiftly. During that time the little band of followers of this new Master had met with him frequently and heard from his lips such gracious words as nothing on earth, nor yet in heaven, could ever efface from their memories.

Blessed meetings! Blessed memories! His way had been made plain to them. Their leader was going away — and not this time through the gateway of death. God be thanked that that horror was not to be relived! The grave had held him once for a few hours and thereby sweetened the ground forever for the dust of all his followers, but never again could earth be so honored. Still, he was going away.

There came a morning when they gathered quietly from hamlet and hillside to an appointed place for that wonderful farewell meeting. What words he spoke to them that day can be learned only from them when the veil of the flesh shall have been removed, and we are privileged to speak with them face-to-face. Oh, those last words of blessing! How they must have engraved themselves upon those loyal hearts!

What we do know is that suddenly, as they watched awestricken and breathless, he began to climb the invisible stairs of the celestial city and went up and *up* and UP, until a pitying cloud, understanding that human eyes and human brains could endure no more, received him out of their sight!

Did they mourn and weep, you ask, and beat the ground in their misery and rend the earth with their cries? I tell you, nay! They went joyfully home, as those who had bidden a brief farewell to a Conqueror who had planned the way they were to follow him in to triumph and to glory.

Such a meeting as his followers held during the ten following days has no parallel in history. They were under orders. They were told to gather and pray and "wait for the promise of the Father." He had promised to send to them a Comforter who would never die, whom the officials could not touch with their venom. This Comforter would stay with them forever, always speaking softly to them about their Master, always luring them forward to the blessed day when he should come again. Aye, he was coming again! "In like manner as they had seen him go" — that was the promise. Then indeed would be established that glorious kingdom for which they had longed. At *last* they understood.

Moreover, they understood their part of the work. They were by no means to be idle while they waited. Every one of them had been commissioned by the Master. They were to be his witnesses on earth, to tell his story and try to lead others to understand and accept adoption into the family of their King.

It was nearly three weeks after that wonderful meeting, the story of which one would like to linger over but must not, that David Holman went home. It was an entirely unexpected action on his part and was the result of a letter from his father that read: "We would like to see you at home at your earliest convenience."

This was sufficiently noncommittal to allow food for all sorts of conjecture. He had not heard from any of the family since Margaret's visit, which had been only of two or three days' duration. He wrote regularly to his mother and sisters but had hardly expected a response. He knew his father too well for that. He had felt almost as much separated from his home as though the ocean rolled between them instead of a few easily traveled miles.

He tossed down the message and began preparations for leaving at once. His rapidly beating heart told him his mother must be very ill. Nothing less than that, he thought, would have drawn a letter from his father.

At evening he reached the house. It was lighted as usual, and there was about it no mysterious something that heralds serious illness. He breathed more freely. From the little parlor issued the sound of voices in earnest conversation. He stepped into the hall very quietly and had his first view of the family unobserved.

His mother was sitting a little in the shadow. His father was in the full light of the lamp, and his face was set in its sternest lines. The girls were also present. No one of them was ill, then. But why had he been sent for?

Then he gave his attention to a guest who seemed to be entertaining the family group. His words flowed on continuously. Undoubtedly the voice was that of Felix Masters. They two could hardly be welcome in the same house! The thought crossed David's mind that possibly he had been sent for to see if this man's matchless logic could not now bring him to his senses. He smiled gravely at the idea. Felix Masters could not hurt him except through his mother and sisters.

Frances turned suddenly toward the hall, and he was discovered.

"Did you drop from the clouds?" asked Margaret, when the initial excitement was over.

But it was the father who replied. "I sent for David, Margaret. But I did not expect him before tomorrow. He must have made good speed. Mr. Masters, we interrupted you. My son will be interested to hear what you were saying."

"Are you quite sure?" asked Mr. Masters. His words seemed to cover a sneer.

Then he addressed himself to David. "We were speaking of the latest developments connected with the curious fanatical outbreak in our city. I was explaining what I feared would be the result. Miss Frances was asking questions about those wonderful meetings that have supposedly been held. Perhaps you are better posted than I and can give us all light."

David's voice was never quieter. "I do not think

human speech can do justice to the meetings," he said, exactly as one would speak who felt that his audience was in utmost sympathy. "They have been simply wonderful. Literally thousands have joined us. From being a little band, as we were when our Leader was here in visible presence, we already number over five thousand and are daily joined by more."

"You have adopted the language of the group, I perceive," said Mr. Masters. This time there was an unmistakable sneer.

It was Frances who interrupted his further speech.

CHAPTER XXIX

THEREFORE WILL NOT WE FEAR

he end seems inadequate to the means, doesn't it?" she asked. "After a few months in the neighborhood a poor stranger gathered a handful of followers, most of them from the ranks of what are called the common people. Inoffensive as he was, doing only kindnesses wherever he went, he somehow secured the hatred of those in power and was speedily put out of the way.

"Yet with what result? The fanaticism has suddenly spread until the entire city is roused, and the followers of this man are counted by thousands instead of by dozens! Many of them are substantial people, I'm told — by no means to be counted among the 'rabble,' which has been such a favorite

ISABELLA MACDONALD ALDEN

word to apply to them before now.

"I wonder how it is all to be accounted for? And I wonder what you officials are going to do about it? You fancied that you had disposed of the leader, and here are his followers increasing in a single day a hundredfold."

David was almost as much astonished as their guest. He had never before heard Frances speak in that calm, cold tone. He hesitated over just what to say. As Mr. Masters did not gather his wits for speech, he turned to Frances with a grave smile.

"People do not understand," David said. "If they could realize that even such a formidable enemy as the grave had no power over our Leader, except for the brief time he chose to have it so, and that he lives today and shall live forever and lead his followers to final victory, then the knowledge would take hold of them with such power that it would revolutionize their lives." He could not tell how his father would listen to such words. But he had been summoned here, and he was a witness.

Mr. Masters found his voice. "I beg your pardon," he said hurriedly. "Can it be that you are in collusion with this unparalleled piece of knavery? Of course, you do not actually *believe* that the man whom the authorities caused to be executed according to the law and who was laid in the grave by some of his own followers really came to life and appeared again on earth!"

David looked at his questioner with steady, quiet eyes. "What do you believe?" he asked. "Did you visit that empty grave, Mr. Masters, and note the useless grave clothes folded there? Did you consult the panic-stricken guard of soldiers? What do you believe about it?"

"Believe!" repeated Felix Masters with his most

hateful sneer. "Why, my dear sir, the veriest child on the streets knows what to believe. It is simple enough. An almost ludicrous combination of knavery and folly. The body was stolen, of course, by some of his sharp friends who have concocted this precious story. The grave clothes, of which you make so much, were left with a purpose evidently, since those in collusion with this remarkable deception are always pushing them to the front."

"And the guard of soldiers," said David, still very quietly. "Have they been punished in accordance with the law for their unparalleled unfaithfulness to their trust? And that large company of people who saw and heard the dead after he had returned to life; who walked with him, talked with him, dined with him and received from his lips the orders which will henceforth control their lives — men like Mr. Rothwell and others of like character, whom you know I could name — have they all suddenly become utterly untrustworthy?"

Mr. Masters lost every vestige of self-control. "Confound them all!" he said, his voice rising. "Masses of them are dupes led on by a few consummate liars. Why did we never see this mysterious person who 'walked and talked and dined' with you? Why was it that though we set guards on every side and watched day and night, we never caught so much as a glimpse of him? The story is not worthy of your usual sharpness, Holman. It would not be believed by a ten-year-old boy, unless he wished to make capital out of it."

"Mr. Masters, may not the officers, who were set to guard every point, have been like those soldiers who guarded the grave? They, you say, permitted a few desolate, unarmed men to rob the grave and carry away the body! May not the other watchmen have permitted our friend to pass? You evidently do not trust your watchmen."

David could not resist this bit of sarcasm. But what reply would have been made will not be known, for it was Margaret Holman who suddenly came to the front, her face pale with indignation.

"Father," she said, "must we all sit here and hear our brother insulted? Mr. Masters has, at least twice, much more than hinted that David was in collusion with people whose deliberate intention was to plan an awful lie for the purpose of deceiving. Now, whatever may be said of others, we certainly know our own. Must we patiently endure such language as this?"

Had she been looking at David, she would have seen his eyes flash with joy.

But Mr. Masters spoke hastily. "I beg your pardon, Miss Margaret, but you misunderstood me. I have always taken the ground that your brother was among the deceived. I have marveled at it, but I did not mean to convey the impression that he was himself an imposter. My language may have been too strong."

"I think it was," said Margaret coldly. "And I don't think you have improved it. I want to make an explanation just here, or a confession. I myself am one of those dupes. I believe in the man you call an imposter, believe in him with all my soul.

"If you would like to know what first opened my eyes to the sin of the course you pursued regarding him, it was the unparalleled cruelty you officers of the law not only permitted toward the prisoner, but furthered. It was also the farce you called a trial. Why, Mr. Masters, a boy of ten could laugh at the folly of calling it 'justice,' when you broke almost every law in your code to hurry it through. As I watched these things and studied and weighed them, I said to myself, They are not punishing a traitor. They are trying to get rid of a man they fear and hate. And my eyes were opened very widely. I am one of the 'traitors.' "

"Thank God!" exclaimed David Holman, springing to his feet. "The joy of this outweighs all my suffering." As he spoke he crossed the room to Margaret and, bending down, kissed her earnestly.

Then, while their dumbfounded guest seemed to be trying to decide what he could say next, the elder Mr. Holman cleared his voice and spoke with the slowness that characterized his deliberate acts. "Mr. Masters, we should perhaps apologize for anything that may seem discourteous to you. My daughter Margaret is very excited. I didn't know her position. I've heard it for the first time from her lips tonight. I think she had some provocation for the words she used about you. But I have more toleration for them than can be expected of her, for I know to what length a blind prejudice will lead one. I know you expected to find an ally in me.

"I should, perhaps, have told you at the beginning of this interview what I want to say now: A great and, I believe, lasting change has come to me. I don't pretend to be wise, but some things I *know*. My son's words about that empty grave are true. I have seen that man, Mr. Masters, and felt his power. I have the light that comes only from him burning in my soul at this moment.

"So not only my son and daughters, but their father and mother, have cast in their lots with him and are to be numbered henceforth among those who follow where he leads. I sent for my son in order to tell him this, but I had planned to do it in a different way."

David made the only response that would have been possible at that moment: "Oh, Father! May we all kneel down and speak to Him?" And while David Holman was praying as he had never prayed before, the guest slipped away. In the intense joy of the moment he had been forgotten. When they arose from their knees, they were alone, and the street door was closed.

The following evening David spent in his room writing to Miriam. The letter was long and took much thought and prayer. At first he had meant to call upon her and say what he feared he could not make plain enough in writing. Then, remembering how impossible it had been to talk plainly to her, he had resolved upon the written attempt.

During all those wonderful weeks that he had been living his new life, anchored and centered in his risen Savior, Miriam had been out of town. He had received a tenderly written note from her, signed, "As ever, your Miriam." It had informed him she was going to spend a few weeks with an invalid friend who needed her.

In the solitude of his own room David's face had flushed over the instant relief that came to him at the thought that they were not in the same city. But this, he assured himself afterward, was because he did not yet know what course to pursue. Now his way was clear. Miriam had chosen to hold him, or rather to recall him, to a pledge that she had herself broken; he was therefore bound, but he must be true. She must have understood what she was doing and what life he must henceforth lead.

"It is as though I had lived years since I last saw you," the letter read. "Then I was under the influence of a great sorrow and disappointment. I felt bewildered at times. Now life spreads before me as clear as sunlight.

"Miriam, in that last talk we had, you remember you told me you would make no more effort to turn my thoughts from the Master I had chosen. I didn't know then what a blessed, glorious Master he is. I know now that I give all my powers joyfully to his service; I am henceforth to live to proclaim his name to others.

"It is due you that I tell you at once that I have given up all idea of the law as a profession. I am to become a preacher of the truth — the truth as it is embodied in our risen Savior. It is to be my daily joy to help others know him.

"I need scarcely tell you how earnestly I long for the time when I may claim you among those who are constantly coming into a knowledge of the truth. I hope and pray that I may be the one to show you the beauty of his life and the power of his resurrection.

"I ask you, Miriam, to join with me in my life-work as I have described it. Remember that you would not feel conspicuous or lonely anymore. Hundreds, no, thousands, many of them your neighbors and acquaintances, have accepted the risen Master as their King."

There was much more to it. He spent more than half the night with her in imagination, going over the story, making it as sweet as an earnest heart given over to the love of it could make it sound to another. As he wrote, the conviction grew upon him that she must not resist his appeal. Aside from her own personal safety and happiness, she must not for his sake. He was bound to her by the strongest cords of honor. How could he do his work well with a divided life?

And then he groaned in spirit and told his awakened conscience for the hundredth time that if he had been truly alive, he would not have sought to join to his a life that was out of accord. What need was there, however, to travel over that ground? He had asked Miriam to be his wife. She had been his deliberate choice, and she held him to the pledge. She had a right to do it. The Master would not let him spoil his life nor hers. He was doing right; the Master would guide.

The morning of a new day was upon him before he sealed his letter. He arose from his knees to do it. Much of his future usefulness depended, humanly speaking, upon its reply; so he believed. He must wait.

Through the long days he waited. Eager to be at work and yearning to join his friends in town and mature plans for the immediate future, he yet waited. His father's work pressed as usual, and he found plenty to occupy him. He also found great joy in the long conversations he held with his father and mother; herein he began his lifework and taught to eager ears the beautiful new truths that had been revealed to him. In truth, the little family had reason to recall these weeks of waiting as a time when they tasted daily of what the coming heaven would be.

Philip Nelson, meanwhile, came and went quite as he used to do in the old days. No, not quite, either. The greeting the father extended him held a quiet sense of satisfaction, such as there had not been before. Mr. Holman was not a man who did anything halfheartedly. It gave him a peculiar sense of joy that he was to have not only a son, but a son-in-law, whose lifework was to direct others to the Master he had himself chosen.

Only Frances knew for what the son waited. The

father and mother were curious, perhaps, but not questioning. They had learned to trust this son of theirs, not only his heart, but his judgment.

"He would make a splendid businessman," the father would say when having a bit of talk with his wife. She felt her heart glow with joy over the contentment in his tone as he added: "But he is going to be something better than that."

Perhaps it was Frances who waited most breathlessly for the reply to that letter. Her brother had learned a lesson of trust.

It is true that, as the days passed and no answer came, he asked himself what the next step should be if he received no word. But immediately he told himself that of course Miriam would write or would send for him. Had she not recalled him when there was no occasion for her to do so? Had she not written to him even after that last interview and signed herself, "As ever, your Miriam." Of course she would make some response. It was like Miriam, perhaps, to wait and weary his soul with conjectures.

He chided himself sternly for admitting so much and then set about apologizing for her. She had been disappointed, doubtless, in his change of life-work. She had always wanted him to be a lawyer. He must give her time to get used to the thought of that and other changes.

At last the response came. They were at the breakfast table when the letters were brought in.

Margaret was curious over David's, but he left the table with it still unopened. An hour afterward he brought its contents to show to Frances. It was the formal announcement of the marriage of Felix Masters and Miriam Brainard Brownlee.

"Thank God!" exclaimed Frances. "Margaret is

saved. And you — oh, David, when I think of you I cannot help saying it again, thank God!"

Months later they were standing together on the vine-wreathed porch of the Rothwell home, David and Mary Holman. They had come back there for a few days of rest after a season of eager work. Their minds that evening were busy with memories.

"Do you remember," said Mary, as her eyes rested on the lush, green vines, "that night when he said, 'I am the vine; you are the branches'? It is good to belong to such a Vine, David."

"Aye," said David, "and I remember when he said, 'Let not your heart be troubled.' I am trying to keep that word with me during these threatening days. Danger is before us, Mary. I feel it in the air, and I admit I tremble sometimes for you. That man Masters and his wife are very busy and shrink at nothing. And the young man, their friend, whom we saw last week, is ready to persecute even to the death all who bear the name of Christian. I saw Stephen, a young friend of mine, this afternoon and tried to warn him. I am sure he is in special danger."

"But Stephen is not afraid, is he?"

"Oh! Stephen lives on the mountaintop. His face made me think of the Master's. But that is one reason why they will hate him more."

There was silence for a moment.

Then Mary said, as she tightened her hold upon his arm, "Oh, David! Can we not rejoice if we shall be counted worthy to suffer for his name's sake?"

"Yes," David assured her, "we will be ready. And so that we may be, we must ever keep before us his last word, 'Lo, I am with you always, even unto the end of the world.' "